HARCOURT
Science

Harcourt School Publishers

Orlando • Boston • Dallas • Chicago • San Diego

www.harcourtschool.com

The **panther chameleon** (*Chamaeleo pardalis*) is native to the eastern and northern coasts of Madagascar and some surrounding islands. The panther chameleon lives in hot, humid rain forests and it eats insects. It can grow to be as long as 30 cm (about 1 ft). It feeds by capturing insects with a sticky tongue that can be as long as its entire body. The tongue can extend out and capture an insect in less than 1/16th of a second. The inside covers of this book show a closeup of the skin of the panther chameleon.

Printed in the United States of America

ISBN	0-15-325389-4	UNIT A
ISBN	0-15-325390-8	UNIT B
ISBN	0-15-325391-6	UNIT C
ISBN	0-15-325392-4	UNIT D
ISBN	0-15-325393-2	UNIT E
ISBN	0-15-325394-0	UNIT F

7 8 9 10 11 12 13 032 10 09 08 07 06 05

Authors

Marjorie Slavick Frank
Former Adjunct Faculty Member
Hunter, Brooklyn, and
    Manhattan Colleges
New York, New York

Robert M. Jones
Professor of Education
University of Houston–
    Clear Lake
Houston, Texas

Gerald H. Krockover
*Professor of Earth and Atmospheric
    Science Education*
School Mathematics and
    Science Center
Purdue University
West Lafayette, Indiana

Mozell P. Lang
Science Education Consultant
Michigan Department
    of Education
Lansing, Michigan

Joyce C. McLeod
Visiting Professor
Rollins College
Winter Park, Florida

Carol J. Valenta
*Vice President—Education, Exhibits,
    and Programs*
St. Louis Science Center
St. Louis, Missouri

Barry A. Van Deman
*Program Director, Informal Science
    Education*
Arlington, Virginia

UNIT A

LIFE SCIENCE

Living Systems

UNIT B LIFE SCIENCE
Systems and Interactions in Nature

UNIT C EARTH SCIENCE
Processes That Change the Earth

UNIT D EARTH SCIENCE

The Solar System and Beyond

PHYSICAL SCIENCE

Building Blocks of Matter

UNIT E

UNIT F

PHYSICAL SCIENCE

Energy and Motion

Planning an Investigation

How do scientists answer a question or solve a problem they have identified? They use organized ways called **scientific methods** to plan and conduct a study. They use science process skills to help them gather, organize, analyze, and present their information.

Justin is using this scientific method for experimenting to find an answer to his question. You can use these steps, too.

STEP 1 Observe and ask questions.

- Use your senses to make observations.
- Record **one** question that you would like to answer.
- Write down what you already know about the topic of your question.
- Decide what other information you need.
- Do research to find more information about your topic.

What design of paper airplane will fly the greatest distance? I need to find out more about airplane wings.

STEP 2 Form a hypothesis.

- Write a possible answer to your question. A possible answer to a question that can be tested is a **hypothesis**.
- Write your hypothesis in a complete sentence.

My hypothesis is: This airplane, with the narrow wings, will fly farthest.

STEP 3 Plan an experiment.

- Decide how to conduct a fair test of your hypothesis by controlling variables. **Variables** are factors that can affect the outcome of the investigation.
- Write down the steps you will follow to do your test.
- List the equipment you will need.
- Decide how you will gather and record your data.

I'll launch each airplane three times. Each airplane will be launched from the same spot, and I'll use the same amount of force each time.

STEP 4 Conduct the experiment.

- Follow the steps you wrote.
- Observe and measure carefully.
- Record everything that happens.
- Organize your data so you can study it carefully.

I'll record each distance. Then I'll find the average distance each airplane traveled.

STEP 5 Draw conclusions and communicate results.

- Analyze the data you gathered.
- Make charts, tables, or graphs to show your data.
- Write a conclusion. Describe the evidence you used to determine whether your test supported your hypothesis.
- Decide whether your hypothesis was correct.

My hypothesis was correct. The airplane with the narrow wings flew farthest.

INVESTIGATE FURTHER

What if your hypothesis was correct . . .

You may want to pose another question about your topic that you can test.

What if your hypothesis was incorrect . . .

You may want to form another hypothesis and do a test on a different variable.

I'll test this new hypothesis: The airplane with the narrow wings will also fly for the longest time.

Do you think Justin's new hypothesis will be correct? Plan and conduct a test to find out!

Using Science Process Skills

When scientists try to find an answer to a question or do an experiment, they use thinking tools called **process skills.** You use many of the process skills whenever you speak, listen, read, write, or think. Think about how these students use process skills to help them answer questions, do experiments, and investigate the world around them.

What Greg plans to investigate

Greg is finding leaves in the park. He wants to make collections of leaves that are alike in some way. He looks for leaves of different sizes and shapes.

Process Skills

Observe—use the senses to learn about objects and events

Compare—identify characteristics about things or events to find out how they are alike and different

Measure—compare an attribute of an object, such as its mass, length, or volume, to a standard unit, such as a gram, centimeter, or liter

Classify—group or organize objects or events in categories based on specific characteristics

How Greg uses process skills

He **observes** the leaves and **compares** their sizes, shapes, and colors. He **measures** each leaf with a ruler. Then he **classifies** the leaves, first into groups based on their sizes and then into groups based on their shapes.

What Pilar plans to investigate

It's been raining for part of the week. Pilar wants to know if it will rain during the coming weekend.

How Pilar uses process skills

She **gathers and records data** to make a prediction about the weather. She observes the weather each day of the week and records it. On a chart, she **displays data** she has gathered. On Friday, she **predicts**, based on her observations, that it will rain during the weekend.

Safety in Science

Doing investigations in science can be fun, but you need to be sure you do them safely. Here are some rules to follow.

1 **Think ahead.** Study the steps of the investigation so you know what to expect. If you have any questions, ask your teacher. Be sure you understand any safety symbols that are shown.

2 **Be neat.** Keep your work area clean. If you have long hair, pull it back so it doesn't get in the way. Roll or push up long sleeves to keep them away from your experiment.

3 **Oops!** If you should spill or break something, or get cut, tell your teacher right away.

4 **Watch your eyes.** Wear safety goggles anytime you are directed to do so. If you get anything in your eyes, tell your teacher right away.

5 **Yuck!** Never eat or drink anything during a science activity.

6 **Don't get shocked.** Be especially careful if an electric appliance is used. Be sure that electric cords are in a safe place where you can't trip over them. Don't ever pull a plug out of an outlet by pulling on the cord.

7 **Keep it clean.** Always clean up when you have finished. Put everything away and wipe your work area. Wash your hands.

In some activities you will see these symbols. They are signs for what you need to be safe.

Be especially careful.

Wear safety goggles.

Be careful with sharp objects.

Don't get burned.

Protect your clothes.

Protect your hands with mitts.

CAUTION

Be careful with electricity.

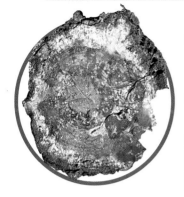

UNIT C — EARTH SCIENCE

Processes That Change the Earth

UNIT EXPERIMENT

Wave Action

Earth's surface is constantly changed by natural processes. One of those processes, the action of waves crashing against a shore, can carry away large quantities of beach sand. While you study this unit, you can conduct a long-term experiment related to this process. Here are some questions to think about. How do artificial structures affect the action of waves? For example, can building jetties stop the loss of beach sand? Plan and conduct an experiment to find answers to these or other questions you have about wave action. See pages x–xvii for help in designing your experiment.

Changes to Earth's Surface

The expression "on solid ground" means that you are certain about something. But there is really no such thing as solid ground—the ground we stand on is always moving.

Fast Fact

In May 1980 Mount St. Helens, a volcano in Washington State, erupted. Ash from the eruption covered an area of more than 22,000 square miles.

There are more than half a million earthquakes every year. Most occur at the bottom of the ocean and are too small to be felt. Only about 1000 earthquakes a year cause any damage.

Fast **Fact**

Mauna Kea, a dormant volcano on the island of Hawai'i, is one of the tallest mountains in the world. From the floor of the Pacific Ocean it rises 9750 m (about 32,000 ft) to sea level and 4205 m (about 13,800 ft) above sea level, for a total height of nearly 14,000 m (about 46,000 ft). By comparison, Mount Everest is 8848 m (about 29,000 ft) high.

LESSON **1**

What Processes Change Landforms?

In this lesson, you can . . .

INVESTIGATE how water cuts through sand.

LEARN ABOUT how wind, water, and ice shape landforms.

LINK to math, writing, social studies, and technology.

▼ Window Rock, Arizona

How Water Changes Earth's Surface

Activity Purpose Moving water is the most powerful force there is for changing Earth's surface. It can move soil, make cliffs fall down, and carve canyons in solid rock. In this investigation, you will **use a model**—a stream table—to **observe** how moving water can cut through sand.

Materials

- stream table
- sand
- 2 lengths of plastic tubing
- 2 plastic pails
- 3 wood blocks
- water

Activity Procedure

1. Place the stream table on a classroom table. Make sure the front end of the stream table is even with the edge of the table. Put the stream-table support under the back end of the stream table. (Picture A)

2. Fill the stream table with sand.

3. Using two fingers, make a path, or channel, down the middle of the sand.

4. Connect one end of one length of tubing to the front of the stream table. Let the other end of the tubing hang over the edge of the table. Place an empty pail on the floor under the hanging end of the tubing. (Picture B)

Picture A

Picture B

5 Place the other pail on two wood blocks near the raised end of the stream-table channel. Fill this pail $\frac{3}{4}$ full of water.

6 Put the second length of tubing into the pail, and fill it with water.

7 Start the water flowing through the tube from the pail to the stream table by lowering one end of the filled tube.

8 **Observe** any changes the water makes to the sand in the stream table. **Record** your observations.

9 Place the third wood block on top of the support under the stream table. Repeat Steps 7 and 8.

Draw Conclusions

1. In which setup was the speed of the water greater?

2. In which setup did you **observe** greater movement of sand from the channel?

3. **Scientists at Work** Scientists learn by **observing**. What did you learn about the way water can change the land by observing the channel in the stream table?

Investigate Further **Hypothesize** what would happen if you replaced the sand with soil. **Plan and conduct a simple experiment** to test your hypothesis.

Process Skill Tip

When you use your eyes to notice how the sand looks before and after water flows through it, you **observe** a change. Careful observations are important in science.

Changes to Earth's Surface

Changing Landforms

FIND OUT

- how Earth's crust is broken down into soil
- how water, wind, and ice change landforms

VOCABULARY

landforms
weathering
erosion
deposition
mass movement

Earth's surface is changing all around you. Rivers wear away rock and produce deep canyons. Waves eat away at sea cliffs, turning them into beach sand. Glaciers scrape away the tops of mountains, and winds carrying sand grind away desert rock. Earth's **landforms**, physical features on its surface, might seem as if they never change, but they do.

In the investigation, you saw how the force of flowing water can move sand. Forces such as flowing water, waves, wind, ice, and even movements inside the Earth are constantly changing landforms. Sometimes the changes happen fast enough for you to observe. For example, a volcano might erupt suddenly and blow away a mountaintop, or a powerful hurricane might sweep away a sandy beach. But most changes to Earth's landforms happen so slowly that you cannot observe them directly. Sometimes you can see only the results of past changes.

✓ **What are some of the forces that change landforms?**

◀ Thousands of years of rain and wind shaped these landforms in Utah's Monument Valley.

Flowing water cuts into riverbanks and carries away soil. ▼

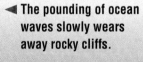

◀ The pounding of ocean waves slowly wears away rocky cliffs.

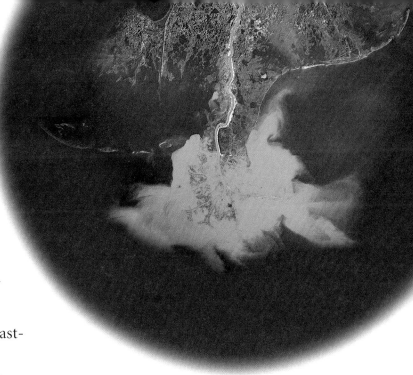

This satellite photo shows the delta the Mississippi River has built in the Gulf of Mexico. ►

Water

Much of Earth's surface is made of rock. The shaping of landforms starts when weathering wears away rock. **Weathering** is the process of breaking rock into silt, sand, clay, and other tiny pieces, called *sediment*. Water is an important agent, or cause, of weathering.

Water weathers rock in several ways. Fast-flowing rivers can carve deep canyons in rock. Arizona's Grand Canyon, carved by the action of the Colorado River, is 1.6 km (about 1 mi) deep. Also, ocean waves can weather cliffs and cause them to fall into the sea. Water can weather rock in other ways, too. When it rains, water seeps into tiny holes, or pores, and cracks in rock. If this water freezes, it expands, breaking the rock. Rain that becomes acidic because of pollution can dissolve rock. And flowing water tumbles rocks against each other, breaking them into smaller pieces and smoothing their edges.

After weathering has broken rock into sediment, erosion and deposition move the sediment around and leave it in new places. **Erosion** (ee•ROH•zhuhn) is the process of moving sediment from one place to another. **Deposition** (dep•uh•ZISH•uhn) is the process of dropping, or depositing, sediment in a new location.

Water is not only an important agent of weathering but also the chief agent of erosion. Water can erode great amounts of sediment. At the shore, sediment from weathered cliffs is eroded by waves and deposited as new sand on beaches. Rainfall erodes sediment and carries it into rivers and streams. Rivers pick up the sediment and move it downstream. Most rivers deposit sediment in flat areas along their banks. These *flood plains*, as they are called, are rich agricultural areas, but they are dangerous places for people to live because of periodic flooding. Some rivers deposit sediment in broad areas at their mouths. These areas of new land are called *deltas*. The Mississippi River delta is one of the largest in the world.

✔ What is the difference between weathering and erosion?

This dam, which forms Lake Lanier in north Georgia, reduces the chances of a damaging flood along the Chattahoochee River. The dam also provides a source of electric energy and recreation. ▼

Wind

Wind is another agent of weathering and erosion. Have you ever seen a machine called a sandblaster? It uses a powerful jet of air containing sand to clean building surfaces. In a similar way, wind can carry bits of rock and sand that weather rock surfaces. Wind also moves sediment from place to place. If the wind blows hard, it can erode a lot of sediment.

In dry areas like the American Southwest, wind erosion has shaped some of the world's most unusual landforms—rocks that look like tables, arches, or columns. Wind erodes dry sediment more easily than it erodes particles of soil or damp rock. And there is little plant life in dry areas to hold sediment in place.

Wind erosion can also blow sand into large mounds called *dunes*. Huge dunes as much as 100 m (about 325 ft) high form in some deserts. Many sandy beaches have long lines of dunes on their land side. Beach dunes are built by the constantly blowing sea breezes. They help protect the land behind them during storms.

✔ **How does wind erosion change landforms?**

Ice

Ice in the form of glaciers can also change landforms. *Glaciers* are thick sheets of ice, formed in areas where more snow falls during the winter than melts during the summer. Glaciers seem to stand still, but they actually move. Because of a glacier's great size and weight, it erodes everything under it. Glaciers erode sediment from one place and deposit it in another.

There are two kinds of glaciers. *Valley glaciers* are found in high mountain valleys. They flow slowly down mountainsides, eroding the mountain under them and forming U-shaped valleys. Only a few valley glaciers remain in North America. And even those are melting rapidly.

Continental glaciers are ice sheets that cover large areas of Earth. They cover almost all of Greenland and Antarctica today. But thousands of years ago, when the climate was colder, continental glaciers covered Europe, Canada, and the northern United States.

✔ **What are glaciers?**

The Athabasca Glacier recedes about 13 m (43 ft) each year. Since 1890, it has receded about 1.6 km (1 mi). ▶

Dunes form where an obstacle, such as a plant or a rock, causes wind to slow and deposit the sand it is carrying. ▼

Sinkhole

◄ The Winter Park sinkhole was large enough to swallow cars and buildings.

▲ Acid rainwater easily dissolves limestone, forming sinkholes.

Mass Movement

During the winter of 1997–1998, heavy rains fell on much of the California coast. One night, families living in a small canyon heard a loud noise. When they went outside to see what had happened, they discovered that a mound of mud had slid down the steep sides of the canyon, covering part of a house. This mudslide occurred when a mass of soil that was full of water moved rapidly downhill.

A mudslide is one type of mass movement. **Mass movement** is the downhill movement of rock and soil because of gravity. Mass movements, such as mudslides and landslides, can change landforms quickly. Mudslides move wet soil. Landslides move dry soil and rock. Landslides occur when gravity becomes stronger than the friction that holds soil in place on a hill. The soil falls suddenly to the bottom of the hill.

Another type of mass movement—one that occurs slowly, as you might guess from its name—is called *creep*. Creep occurs when soil moves slowly downhill because of gravity. Creep is so slow that changes in landforms are hard to observe directly. The land may move only a few centimeters each year. But over time, creep can move fences, utility poles, roads, and railroad tracks.

One day in 1981, in the city of Winter Park, Florida, an area of land suddenly collapsed, or fell in on itself. The hole swallowed houses, swimming pools, and businesses, including a car dealership. Today there is a lake where there was once dry land. The process that led to the formation of the Winter Park sinkhole is different from that of other types of mass movement.

A sinkhole is a large hole in the ground that opens suddenly. Sinkholes form after rock under the surface has dissolved or become weak. Sinkholes often appear in areas of limestone rock, because limestone dissolves easily. Rain seeping into the ground combines with carbon dioxide from the air to form a weak acid called *carbonic acid*. Carbonic acid dissolves limestone, forming huge holes. When enough rock has dissolved, land over the weakened area collapses.

✔ **What is mass movement?**

C9

New Landforms

Erosion and deposition can change landforms or produce new ones. Rivers can deposit sediment that builds deltas. They can also change their path, or course, producing new lakes on wide flood plains.

Glaciers are major forces for forming new landforms. As the glaciers of the last Ice Age moved forward, they pushed mounds of rock and soil in front of them. When the glaciers melted, they left behind at their lower ends long ridges of soil and rock, called *terminal moraines*. Long Island and Cape Cod are terminal moraines. They mark the leading edge of the glacier that covered much of North America.

New islands can be formed by volcanic eruptions. Underwater volcanoes increase their height by depositing melted rock and ash. In time, they build up enough to appear above the sea surface as islands. The Hawaiian Islands formed in this way. Almost constant eruptions of Kīlauea add daily to the size of the island of Hawai'i. Another volcano, now growing slowly on the ocean floor southeast of Hawai'i, will one day become the island of Loihi.

✓ **What new landforms are created by erosion and deposition?**

Old, slow-moving rivers form broad loops. ▼

The loops can become so broad that they meet. ▼

Because the river follows the shortest route, its flow cuts off the loop. The old loop forms a crescent-shaped body of water called an *oxbow lake*. ▼

Mississippi River, south of Memphis, Tennessee ▼

Summary

Weathering breaks down the rock of Earth's surface into soil, sand, and other small particles. Agents of erosion, such as water, wind, and ice, change Earth's landforms by moving rock and soil. Water can carve canyons and deposit sediment to form deltas. Wind can form sand dunes. Ice can carve U-shaped valleys and leave landforms such as terminal moraines. Even forces within the Earth, such as volcanoes, can produce new landforms.

Review

1. What is erosion?
2. What is deposition?
3. What forces cause erosion and deposition?
4. **Critical Thinking** Why is weathering so important to life on land?
5. **Test Prep** A type of mass movement is a —
   A glacier
   B delta
   C mudslide
   D terminal moraine

LINKS

MATH LINK

Organize/Display Data The Aletsch Glacier in Europe is 80 km^2. Malaspina Glacier in Alaska measures 1344 km^2. The Grinnell Glacier in Montana is about 2 km^2. Use a computer, if possible, to make a bar graph that compares these glaciers.

WRITING LINK

Informative Writing—Description During the 1930s huge dust storms eroded large areas of the Great Plains of the United States. Find out what caused the Dust Bowl, as the eroded region was called, and what problems it led to. Then describe how modern farming practices, such as contour plowing, can help prevent soil erosion.

SOCIAL STUDIES LINK

Topographic Maps Topographic maps use symbols and colors to represent landforms. These maps can tell you how the land looks—if you know how to read them. At the library, look for a topographic map of the area where you live. What kinds of symbols are used to show water, wetlands, and deserts?

TECHNOLOGY LINK

Learn more about landscapes and erosion by visiting this Internet site.
www.scilinks.org/harcourt

SCiLINKS
THE WORLD'S A CLICK AWAY

LESSON 2

What Causes Mountains, Volcanoes, and Earthquakes?

In this lesson, you can . . .

INVESTIGATE the structure of Earth.

LEARN ABOUT what forms mountains and volcanoes.

LINK to math, writing, literature, and technology.

Volcanoes release melted rock from deep inside Earth. ▼

INVESTIGATE

Journey to the Center of Earth

Activity Purpose If you could slice Earth in half, you would see that it has several layers. Of course, you can't slice Earth in half, but you can make a model of it. In this investigation you will **make a model** that shows Earth's layers.

Materials

- 2 graham crackers
- 1 small plastic bag
- disposable plastic gloves
- 1 spoon
- 1 jar peanut butter
- 1 hazelnut or other round nut
- freezer
- plastic knife

Activity Procedure

1. Put the graham crackers in the plastic bag. Close the bag and use your hands to crush the crackers into crumbs. Then set the bag aside.

2. Put on the plastic gloves. Use the spoon to scoop a glob of peanut butter from the jar and put it in your gloved hand. Place the nut in the center of the peanut butter. Cover the nut with more peanut butter until there is about 2.5 cm of peanut butter all around the nut. Using both hands, roll the glob of peanut butter with the nut at its center into a ball. (Picture A)

Picture A

Picture B

3 Open the bag of crushed graham crackers, and roll the peanut butter ball in the graham cracker crumbs until the outside of the ball is completely coated.

4 Put the ball in the freezer for about 15 minutes. Remove the ball and cut into your model with the plastic knife. **Observe** the layers inside. You might want to take a photograph of your model for later review. (Picture B)

Draw Conclusions

1. The peanut butter ball is a model of Earth's layers. How many layers does Earth have in this model?

2. Which layer of Earth do the crushed graham crackers represent? Why do you think your model has a thick layer of peanut butter but a thin layer of graham cracker crumbs?

3. **Scientists at Work** Scientists can see and understand complex structures better by **making models** of them. What does the model show about Earth's layers? What doesn't the model show about Earth's layers?

Investigate Further Some geologists, scientists who study the Earth, say that Earth's center is divided into a soft outer part and a hard inner part. How could you **make a model** to show this?

Process Skill Tip

You cannot see Earth's layers. So **making a model** helps you understand how they look in relation to each other. In this activity, you need to cut open the model to see the layers.

Mountains, Volcanoes, and Earthquakes

FIND OUT

- how mountains form
- what causes volcanoes and earthquakes

VOCABULARY

crust
mantle
core
plate
magma
volcano
earthquake
fault

Earth's Interior

As the model you made in the investigation showed, Earth is not a solid ball of rock. It has three distinct layers. We live on Earth's crust. The **crust** is the outer layer, and it is made of rock. Earth's crust is very thin compared to the other layers. If Earth were the size of a chicken's egg, the crust would be thinner than the egg's shell.

The **mantle** is the layer of rock beneath Earth's crust. Just under the crust, the rock of the mantle is solid. But the mantle is very hot. This makes part of the mantle soft, like melted candy. No one has ever been to the mantle, but rock from the mantle sometimes reaches Earth's surface through volcanoes.

The **core** is the center layer of Earth. It is Earth's hottest layer. The core can be divided into two parts: an outer core of liquid, or *molten,* iron and an inner core of solid iron. Even though the core is very hot, great pressure at the center of Earth keeps the inner core solid.

✔ **What parts of Earth are solid?**

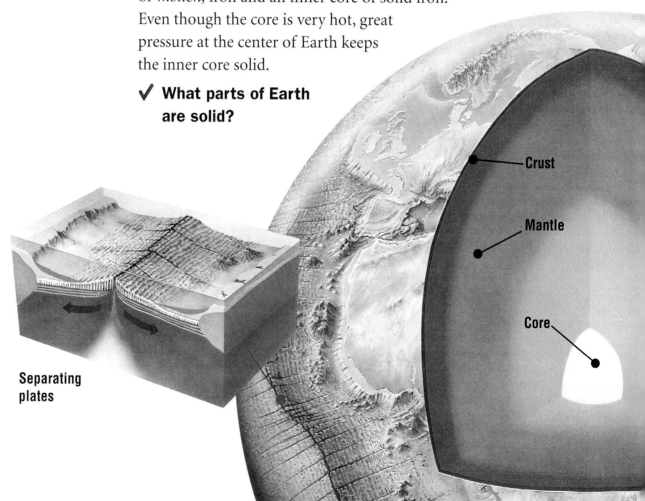

Separating plates

Crust

Mantle

Core

Earth's Crust Moves

Earth's surface is not a single piece of rock. Instead, it is made up of many plates. **Plates** are rigid blocks of crust and upper mantle rock. Most of North America, Greenland, and the western half of the North Atlantic Ocean are on the North American plate. Part of California and most of the Pacific Ocean make up the Pacific plate. There are 12 major plates in all. Earth's plates fit together like the pieces of a jigsaw puzzle.

Although these plates are enormous, they actually float on the soft rock of the mantle. Pressure and heat within the Earth produce currents in the soft rock of the mantle. As the mantle moves, the plates floating on it move, too.

Plate movement is very slow—only a few centimeters each year. But because plates are right next to each other, the movement of one plate affects other plates. Some plates push together. Some pull apart. Other plates slide past each other. As plates move around, they cause great changes in Earth's landforms.

Where plates collide, energy is released, and new landforms are produced. On land, mountains rise and volcanoes erupt. South America's Andes Mountains are a result of the Nazca and South American plates colliding. On the ocean floor, deep trenches form.

As plates pull apart on land, valleys dotted with volcanoes develop. Africa's Great Rift Valley was formed by the African and Arabian plates pulling apart. The rift, or crack, will one day result in a complete separation of part of eastern Africa from the rest of the continent. Where plates pull apart under the sea, ridges and volcanoes form. This spreading forms new sea floor at the ridges.

When plates scrape and slide past each other, they shake Earth's surface. Along the San Andreas (an•DRAY•uhs) fault in California, the Pacific plate is moving past the North American plate. As the plates grind past each other, they sometimes slip, causing earthquakes.

✔ **What are Earth's plates?**

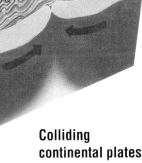

Colliding ocean plates

Colliding continental plates

The Himalayas formed as the Indian plate pushed into the Eurasian plate. The plates are still pushing together, and the mountains are still getting taller.

Mountain Formation

Mountains are Earth's highest landforms. They form as the crust folds, cracks, and bends upward because of the movements of Earth's plates.

Many of the highest mountains form where continental plates collide. As the plates push together, their edges crumple and fold into mountains. The Himalayas (him•uh•LAY•uhz), Earth's highest mountain range, formed this way.

At some places, continental and oceanic plates collide. Because continental rock is less dense than seafloor rock, the continental plate moves up and over the oceanic plate. The Cascade Mountains, near the Pacific Ocean, formed this way.

Mountains do not form only at the edges, or boundaries, of plates. Some mountains form where pressure from movement at the boundaries pushes a block of rock upward. The Grand Tetons (TEE•tahnz) of Wyoming rise straight up from the flat land around them.

Plates that pull apart leave gaps between them. Magma bubbles up between the plates. **Magma** is molten rock from Earth's mantle. Magma builds up along the cracks, forming long chains of mountains under

the ocean. These mountains are called *mid-ocean ridges*. The Mid-Atlantic Ridge is Earth's longest mountain range. It separates the North American and Eurasian plates in the North Atlantic and the South American and African plates in the South Atlantic.

✔ **How do many of the highest mountains form?**

Volcanoes

You have read that most volcanoes form at plate boundaries. A **volcano** is a mountain formed by lava and ash. *Lava* is magma that reaches Earth's surface. *Ash* is small pieces of hardened lava.

Chains of volcanoes form where a continental plate and an oceanic plate collide. The edge of the oceanic plate pushes under the edge of the continental plate. The leading edge of the oceanic plate melts as it sinks deep into the mantle. The melted rock becomes magma that forces its way up between the plates. The volcanoes of the Cascades, such as Mount St. Helens, formed this way.

Sometimes volcanoes form in the middle of plates, over unusually hot columns of magma. The magma melts a hole in the plate and rises through the hole, causing a volcanic eruption. The Hawaiian Islands are the tops of a chain of volcanoes that formed in the middle of the Pacific plate. As the Pacific plate continues moving over this hot spot, new volcanoes and new islands form. The big island of Hawai'i, with its active volcanoes, Kilauea and Mauna Loa, is the youngest island in the chain. Kure Atoll, an extinct volcano 2617 km (about 1625 mi) to the northwest, is the oldest island.

✔ **What is a volcano?**

▲ Many volcanoes are located at plate boundaries around the Pacific plate. That's why this area is called the Ring of Fire.

THE INSIDE STORY

Volcanoes

Volcanoes take on their characteristic shapes as lava and ash build up around their openings, or *vents*.

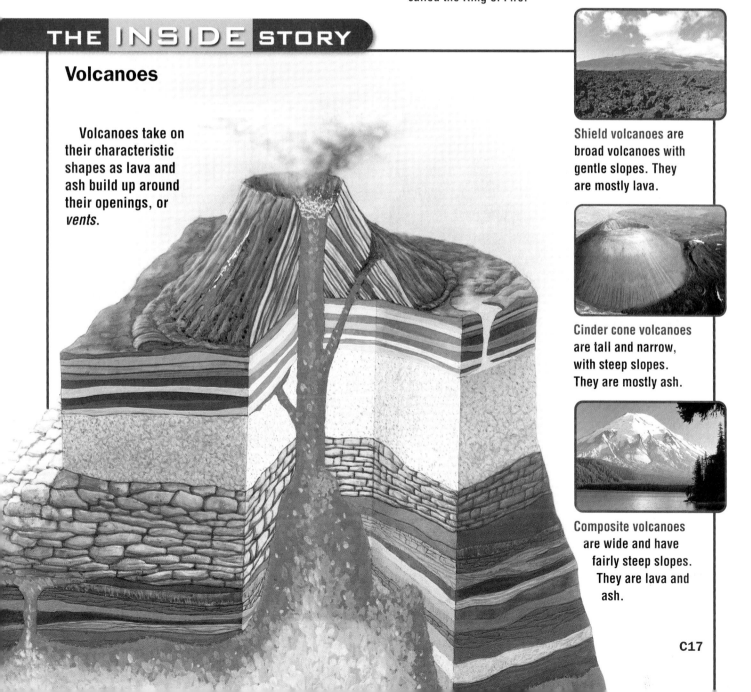

Shield volcanoes are broad volcanoes with gentle slopes. They are mostly lava.

Cinder cone volcanoes are tall and narrow, with steep slopes. They are mostly ash.

Composite volcanoes are wide and have fairly steep slopes. They are lava and ash.

In 1964 a large earthquake hit Anchorage, Alaska. Streets split open, bridges collapsed, and houses slid downhill toward the sea.

Earthquake center, or *focus*

Fault

Earthquakes

On March 27, 1964, thousands of people in Anchorage, Alaska, were shaken as the ground rocked under them. A strong earthquake, possibly the most powerful one ever recorded, knocked down houses, broke up roads, and cut water, gas, and power lines all over the area.

An **earthquake** is a shaking of the ground caused by the sudden release of energy in Earth's crust. The energy released as plates crush together, scrape past each other, or bend along jagged boundaries can cause great damage. Earthquakes are very

common. More than a million of them occur each year. However, most are too small to be felt or to cause damage.

Many earthquakes occur along the boundaries of the Pacific plate. Earthquakes also occur along faults in the crust. You have read that Earth's crust can bend or break in the middle of a plate as forces press in on it. These breaks can form **faults**, or places where pieces of the crust move.

An earthquake sends out energy in the form of *seismic* (SYZ•mik) *waves*. Seismic waves are like ripples that form on a pond when a stone is tossed in. Scientists measure and record seismic waves on an instrument called a *seismograph* (SYZ•muh•graf). These measurements can then be used to compare the relative strengths of earthquakes.

Major Earthquakes

Magnitude	Year	Location
9.2	1964	Alaska
8.9	1933	Japan
8.4	1946	Japan
8.2	1976	China
8.1	1979	Indonesia
8.1	1985	Mexico
7.9	2001	India
6.9	1989	California

▲ The Richter scale is often used to measure relative strengths, or *magnitudes,* of earthquakes. On this scale an earthquake with a magnitude of 7.5, for example, is 32 times more powerful than an earthquake with a magnitude of 6.5.

✔ **What is an earthquake?**

◀ Sudden movement along a fault can cause an earthquake.

Summary

Earth has three layers: the crust, the mantle, and the core. Rock of the crust and upper mantle makes up plates that fit together like puzzle pieces. Earth's plates collide, pull apart, and slide past each other. Most mountains and volcanoes form at plate boundaries. Many earthquakes also occur at plate boundaries.

Review

1. Describe three ways in which Earth's plates interact.
2. What is magma and where does it come from?
3. How do volcanoes form where oceanic and continental plates collide?
4. **Critical Thinking** Assume that the overall size of Earth's crust stays the same. If one plate is pushing away from the plate next to it on one side, what must be happening at the boundary with another plate on the opposite side?
5. **Test Prep** Many strong earthquakes are caused by —
   A plates sliding past each other
   B lava flowing down the side of a volcano
   C plates spreading apart
   D hot magma

LINKS

MATH LINK

Estimate Each whole number on the Richter scale represents a force 32 times as strong as the next lower number. An earthquake of magnitude 7 is about 32 times as strong as one of magnitude 6. About how many times as strong is an earthquake of magnitude 8 compared with an earthquake of magnitude 5?

WRITING LINK

Informative Writing—Explanation The 1980 explosion of Mount St. Helens was a very powerful volcanic eruption. Find pictures in books and magazines of Mount St. Helens before, during, and after the eruption. Write captions for the pictures to explain what happened. Share your photo essay with your class.

LITERATURE LINK

Volcano: The Eruption and Healing of Mount St. Helens by Patricia Lauber (Bradbury Press, 1986) explains how and why Mount St. Helens erupted. It also describes the destruction the eruption caused, and how the land has since recovered.

TECHNOLOGY LINK

Learn more about volcanoes by viewing *Ring of Fire* and *Volcano Hunters* on the **Harcourt Science Newsroom Video.**

C19

How Has Earth's Surface Changed?

In this lesson, you can . . .

INVESTIGATE the movement of continents.

LEARN ABOUT how Earth's surface has changed over time.

LINK to math, writing, art, and technology.

◄ Over millions of years, these trees have turned to stone.

INVESTIGATE

Movement of the Continents

Activity Purpose Earth's surface 100 million years ago probably looked much different than it does today. In the last lesson, you read that Earth's surface is made up of plates that move. In this investigation, you will **make a model** to find out how Earth's surface might have looked before these plates moved to their present locations.

Materials

- 3 copies of a world map
- scissors
- 3 sheets of construction paper
- glue
- globe or world map

Activity Procedure

1 Cut out the continents from one copy of the world map.

2 Arrange the continents into one large "supercontinent" on a sheet of construction paper. As you would with a jigsaw puzzle, arrange them so their edges fit together as closely as possible. (Picture A)

3 Label the pieces with the names of their present continents, and glue them onto the paper.

4 Use a globe or world map to locate the following mountains: Cascades, Andes, Atlas, Himalayas, Alps. Then draw these mountains on the supercontinent.

Picture A

Picture B

5 Use your textbook to locate volcanoes and places where earthquakes have occurred. Put a *V* in places where you know there are volcanoes, such as the Cascades. Put an *E* in places where you know that earthquakes have occurred, such as western North America.

6 Repeat Steps 1–5 with the second copy of the world map, but before gluing the continents to the construction paper, separate them by about 2.5 cm. That is, leave about 2.5 cm of space between North America and Eurasia, between South America and Africa, and so on. (Picture B)

7 Glue the third world map copy onto a sheet of construction paper. Then place the three versions of the world map in order from the oldest to the youngest.

Draw Conclusions

1. Where do the continents fit together the best?

2. Where are most of the mountains, volcanoes, and earthquake sites in relation to the present continents? Why do you think they are there?

3. **Scientists at Work** Scientists **use models**, such as maps, to better understand complex structures and processes. How did your models of Earth's continents help you **draw conclusions** about Earth's past? What limitations did your models have?

Investigate Further **Hypothesize** about the fact that the continents do not fit together exactly. Then **plan and conduct a simple investigation** to test your hypothesis.

> **Process Skill Tip**
>
> It is impossible to actually see Earth's surface as it looked millions of years ago. But by **using a model**, you can **draw conclusions** about how it may have looked.

How Earth's Surface Has Changed

Continental Drift

FIND OUT

• how Earth's surface features have changed over millions of years

• how fossils help scientists to learn about plants and animals of the past

VOCABULARY

continental drift
Pangea
fossil

From evidence like the models you used in the investigation, scientists infer that Earth's surface has not always looked the way it does today. The surface is constantly changing because of continental drift. **Continental drift** is the theory of how Earth's continents move over its surface.

According to the theory, about 225 million years ago, all of the land on Earth was joined together in one "supercontinent" called **Pangea** (pan•JEE•uh). Evidence suggests that about 200 million years ago, Pangea broke into two big continents. The southern one, Gondwana, contained all the land that is now in the Southern Hemisphere. The northern continent, Laurasia, contained land that would become North America and Eurasia. Finally, Gondwana and Laurasia broke into smaller land masses, forming the continents we know today.

Since the continents are still moving, you might infer that the surface of Earth will be very different 200 million years from now. The Atlantic Ocean is getting wider, pushing Europe and North America apart. The Pacific Ocean is getting smaller. And Australia is moving north.

✔ **What is the theory of continental drift?**

Continental Drift

200 million years ago
Pangea begins to break apart.

100 million years ago
Gondwana breaks into smaller continents earlier than Laurasia does.

Today
Earth's surface may look even different in the future.

The Rock Record

If you were floating down the Colorado River through the deepest part of the Grand Canyon, shown at the right, you would be looking up at layers of rock nearly 2 billion years old! The Grand Canyon is a mile-deep slice into Earth's history, cutting through 20 different layers of rock.

Some of the rocks of the canyon contain a fossil record of organisms from Earth's early history. **Fossils** are the remains or traces of past life found in some rocks. Scientists study fossils to find out how life on Earth has changed.

Scientists also depend on the fact that some things will always be the same. Processes that produced features like the Grand Canyon are still occurring today. Running water still erodes rock layers, and new layers of rock are still forming from deposited sediments.

From the position of certain rock layers, scientists can infer the relative ages of the rocks. Younger rock layers are found on top of older rock layers. The oldest rock layers are near the bottom of the Grand Canyon.

The walls of the Grand Canyon do not contain rock from the latest stages of Earth's history. Erosion has worn away more recent rock. If you stand on the canyon's north rim, you are standing on rock that is about 250 million years old.

✔ **Why is looking at the Grand Canyon like looking at Earth's history?**

The youngest rocks are at the top of the canyon walls.

The oldest rocks are at the bottom of the canyon.

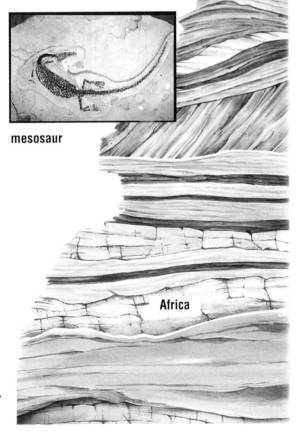

South America

Similar rock layers and similar fossils, such as the mesosaur shown below, have been found in both South America and Africa. This provides evidence that the continents may once have been joined together.

mesosaur

Africa

How Fossils Show Changes

Fossils show us that life on Earth has not always been the same as it is now. Dinosaurs once roamed Earth, as did large, elephantlike animals called *woolly mammoths.* Scientists have drawn conclusions about these creatures from what they left behind—whole mammoths frozen in ice and fossilized bones and teeth of dinosaurs.

Most fossils, however, are not the actual remains of once-living organisms. Instead, they are traces left behind when dead plants and animals decayed or dissolved. When sediment buries an organism, it can produce a mold or cast as the sediment hardens into rock. A mold forms when underground water dissolves the organism, leaving only its shape behind in the rock. If sediments fill the empty space and harden, the fossil becomes a cast.

In addition to showing what kinds of organisms lived on Earth long ago, fossils also show that Earth's surface was different than it is today. Scientists have found fossils of sea organisms in rock at the tops of high mountains. They infer that those rocks were once under water.

Scientists use fossil evidence to support the theory of continental drift. Fossils of similar plants and animals have been found in Africa, South America, India, and Australia. This means that these widely separated continents must have been joined at one time.

✔ **How are fossils used to show changes?**

▲ Scientists called *paleontologists* study fossils to learn about life of the past.

Summary

Earth's continents once were joined to form a supercontinent called Pangea. Pangea broke apart and, over millions of years, the continents drifted to their present locations. Fossils, the remains and traces of dead organisms, show what Earth's life was like in the past. They also show that Earth's surface has changed.

Review

1. What was Pangea?
2. How old are the oldest rocks of the Grand Canyon?
3. How do we know that Earth's life was different in the past?
4. **Critical Thinking** Why is the Grand Canyon important to scientists studying Earth's past?
5. **Test Prep** The Southern continent that existed 200 million years ago was called —

   A Gondwana   C Laurasia
   B Precambria   D Eurasia

LINKS

MATH LINK

Collect/Organize/Display Data
Research Earth's history. Then make a chart showing the relative lengths of various eras. Your chart should show how long each era lasted and how long ago each occurred. Draw the chart to scale. For example, if an era lasted for half the time of Earth's history, it should cover half the chart.

WRITING LINK

Informative Writing—Compare and Contrast You learned that Earth's continents were once in different places. Where will they be in the future? Research what a map of the world might look like 100 million years from now. Then compare and contrast this map with a current map in a report for your teacher.

ART LINK

Past Life Look for illustrations of what Earth's surface might have looked like thousands, or even millions, of years ago. Compare what you find with the way Earth's surface looks today.

TECHNOLOGY LINK

Learn more about changes to Earth's surface by visiting the National Air and Space Museum Internet site.
www.si.edu/harcourt/science

Smithsonian Institution®

Exploring Earth's Surface from Space

This drawing shows a Geosat circling Earth.

Newly released satellite images of the ocean floor are making scientists question old theories about the processes that change Earth's surface.

Satellite Secrets

Until recently, information collected by a U.S. government Geosat satellite was top secret. Now data gathered by this satellite has been released, and geologists are excited. However, they say it will take about ten years to analyze the satellite's images of Earth's geologic processes.

If you've ever sailed on the ocean, you probably couldn't tell that the water bulges up in certain places. It does this because of gravity. Rock on the ocean floor has a gravitational pull for the water around it. The more rock, the stronger the pull. The stronger the pull, the more the water bulges up. A 2000-m (about 6562-ft) underwater volcano causes a water bulge of about 2 m (6.6 ft).

Sensitive equipment on board a Geosat can measure these bulges from space. By measuring the surface of the ocean very precisely, the satellite produces clear gravity images of volcanoes, mountain ranges, plains, and other "landforms" on the ocean floor.

New Data Shakes Up Old Theories

Many areas of the ocean floor had never been surveyed before. About half of the underwater volcanoes shown by the Geosat's gravity imaging had not been known to exist. Gravity images of water bulges are also making scientists question old theories about how volcanic island chains form.

The old theory, called the "hot spot" model, said that there are hot areas in Earth's mantle. As Earth's plates pass slowly

Many of the volcanoes under the Pacific Ocean were discovered by gravity imaging.

over a hot spot, a long line of volcanoes forms. Each new volcano in the line is younger than the one just before it.

But the hot spot model can't explain some of the newly discovered volcano chains. For example, the Pukapuka Ridges, which extend for thousands of kilometers east of Tahiti, seem to have erupted all at the same time. Rock samples from different parts of the chain are all the same age.

Scientists are arguing about what these new discoveries mean in terms of the old theories about hot spots being correct. Many agree that the hot spot model may be wrong. All agree that there is much work ahead to develop more accurate theories based on this Geosat data.

THINK ABOUT IT

1. How does gravity imaging work?
2. Why do you think oil companies might be interested in gravity images?

Kia K. Baptist
GEOSCIENTIST

"A key to being a scientist is to be unafraid to ask questions and unafraid that there may not be answers."

Kia Baptist can see what lies below Earth's surface. She is a geoscientist who works for an oil company. Her job is to help find oil and natural gas resources by finding clues in different kinds of data.

Ms. Baptist collects seismic data by creating small "earthquakes" in rock. Then she analyzes the sound signals that return and uses them to map the rock formations and structures underground.

Ms. Baptist also analyzes geochemical data to learn the chemical nature of the rock. This tells her what kind of rock it is, how old it is, and whether there is oil present. This information, along with computer technology, allows her to give advice to the oil companies on specific locations where oil and natural gas may be found.

Looking for clues is natural for Ms. Baptist. As a child growing up in Baltimore, Maryland, she was a mystery solver. She decided she wanted to help solve the mysteries of space by becoming an astronaut. Several times she worked as an intern at NASA, learning all she could about astronomy and physics. She took courses in many areas of science, believing that knowing about all branches of science would help her do her best work in one. When she began to study geology and chemistry, she realized her true interest lay in those areas. She hasn't stopped studying the Earth since then.

Ms. Baptist gives good advice to young scientists. She says, "Part of the process of science is attacking a problem and trying to find answers, but don't be intimidated if you don't find answers right away. Just keep learning."

THINK ABOUT IT

1. How could analyzing seismic data give clues about where oil is located?

2. Why is it important to know the specific location of oil?

ACTIVITIES FOR HOME OR SCHOOL

MODEL EARTH

How can you model Earth's layers?

Materials

- rounded objects, such as

  an apple
  an avocado
  a peach
  a hard-boiled egg
  a nectarine

  a tennis ball
  an orange
  a plum
  plain chocolates, or
  chocolate-covered
  peanuts

Procedure

❶ Make two columns on a sheet of paper.

❷ Label one column "Does Model Earth's Layers." Label the other column "Does Not Model Earth's Layers."

❸ Decide what characteristics an object must have to model Earth's layers.

❹ Examine each object. Then write the name of the object in the appropriate column.

Draw Conclusions

What characteristics must an object have to model Earth's layers? Which parts of the objects in the "Does Model Earth's Layers" column represent Earth's layers? What other objects can you think of that model Earth's layers?

FEATURING EARTH

How do landforms change?

Materials

- apple
- tape measure
- pan
- hotpad
- oven

Procedure

❶ Measure the circumference of the apple.

❷ Place the apple in a pan and, using the hot pad, put the pan in the oven and bake it for one hour at 300°F.

❸ Your teacher or another adult will remove the apple from the oven. Allow it to cool, and measure it again.

❹ Observe the features of the baked apple.

Draw Conclusions

In some ways, baked apples are a good model of how Earth's landforms change. Compare the circumference of the apple before and after you baked it. What happened to the peel as the apple cooled? What layer of Earth does the peel represent? What "landforms" can you identify on the apple peel? In what ways is the apple not a good model of Earth's changing landforms?

Vocabulary Review

Use the terms below to complete the sentences. The page numbers in ( ) tell you where to look in the chapter if you need help.

landform (C6)
weathering (C7)
erosion (C7)
deposition (C7)
mass movement (C9)
crust (C14)
mantle (C14)
core (C14)
plate (C15)

magma (C16)
volcano (C16)
earthquake (C18)
fault (C18)
continental drift (C22)
Pangea (C22)
fossils (C23)

1. An ____ is a sudden release of energy in Earth's ____, causing the ground to shake.

2. A rigid block of Earth's crust and upper mantle rock is a ____.

3. A ____ is a physical feature on Earth's surface, such as a mountain or valley.

4. The remains or traces of past life found in Earth's crust are called ____.

5. Molten rock from Earth's mantle is ____.

6. A ____ is a break in Earth's crust, along which pieces of the crust move.

7. ____ is the process of breaking rock into silt, sand, and other tiny pieces called sediment.

8. Lava is magma that reaches Earth's surface through an opening, called a ____, in Earth's crust.

9. The downhill movement of rock and soil because of gravity is ____.

10. The ____ is the layer of rock beneath Earth's crust.

11. The theory that the continents move over Earth's surface is ____.

12. ____ is the supercontinent that held all of Earth's land 225 million years ago.

13. ____ is the process of moving sediment from one place to another, and ____ is the process of dropping, or depositing, sediment in a new location.

14. The ____ is the center of Earth.

Connect Concepts

Use the Word Bank to complete the sentences.

deltas   beaches   tables   sinkholes   terminal moraines
arches   canyons   dunes   floodplains

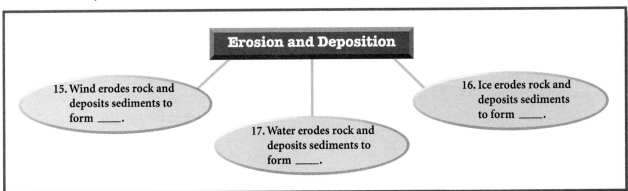

Erosion and Deposition

15. Wind erodes rock and deposits sediments to form ____.

16. Ice erodes rock and deposits sediments to form ____.

17. Water erodes rock and deposits sediments to form ____.

Check Understanding

Write the letter of the best choice.

18. Beginning with the outermost layer, Earth's layers are the —
   A crust, magma, and core
   B crust, mantle, and core
   C core, mantle, and crust
   D core, magma, and crust

19. Gondwana and Laurasia were formed by —
   F continental drift
   G erosion
   H deposition
   J earthquakes

20. Which of the following was **NOT** an ancient continent?
   A Pangea
   B Laurasia
   C Gondwana
   D Cenozoa

Critical Thinking

21. Explain why water erodes Earth's surface more than wind does.

22. If the mantle were solid rock, what feature would not form on Earth's surface? Explain.

23. Scientists have found many fossils of past life. Are fossils still being formed today? Explain.

Process Skills Review

24. What can you **observe** about these pieces of rock that shows you which one has been weathered and moved by water?

25. How might you **make a model** of a volcano?

Performance Assessment

Plate Boundaries

   Identify the three types of plate boundaries at A, B, and C in the illustration below. Explain what is happening at each boundary.

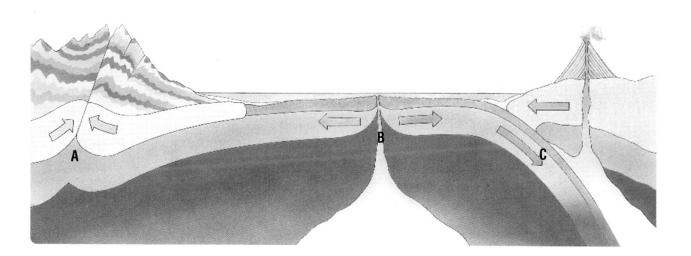

Rocks and Minerals

Rocks and minerals are all around you. The ground you walk on every day is made of rocks and minerals. They are in the soil. They are the gems that sparkle in jewelry. The Earth itself is made mostly of rocks and minerals.

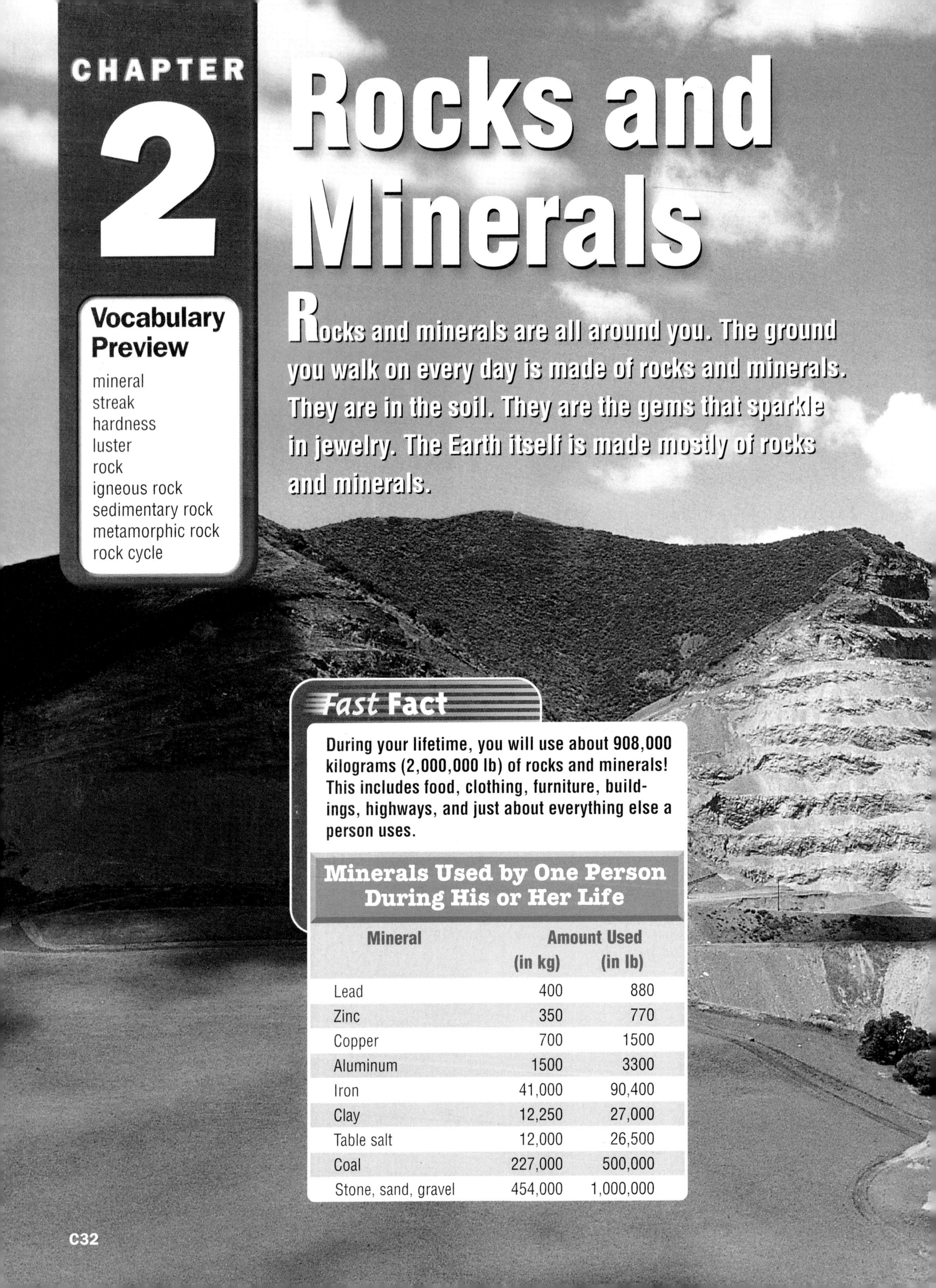

Vocabulary Preview

mineral
streak
hardness
luster
rock
igneous rock
sedimentary rock
metamorphic rock
rock cycle

Fast Fact

During your lifetime, you will use about 908,000 kilograms (2,000,000 lb) of rocks and minerals! This includes food, clothing, furniture, buildings, highways, and just about everything else a person uses.

Minerals Used by One Person During His or Her Life

Mineral	Amount Used (in kg)	(in lb)
Lead	400	880
Zinc	350	770
Copper	700	1500
Aluminum	1500	3300
Iron	41,000	90,400
Clay	12,250	27,000
Table salt	12,000	26,500
Coal	227,000	500,000
Stone, sand, gravel	454,000	1,000,000

All the gold known in the world would fit in a cube measuring about 18 meters (60 ft) on each side! But a little bit goes a long way. Twenty-eight grams (about 1 oz) of gold can be flattened into a thin sheet covering about 28 square meters (300 sq ft). That's enough to cover one-fourth of a tennis court!

These pictures show equal weights of gold and salt. In ancient times, salt was so precious that it was traded ounce for ounce for gold! If you worked hard and you were "worth your salt," you were paid a "salary." This word meant "money for buying salt"!

This gravel quarry provides gravel for roads and buildings.

1

What Are Minerals?

In this lesson, you can . . .

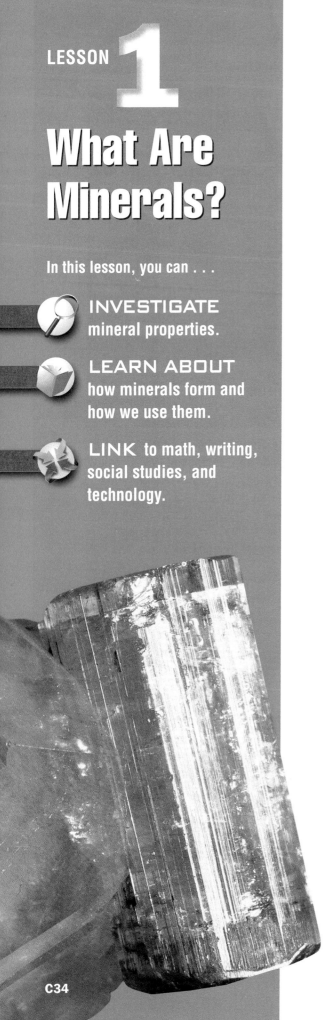

INVESTIGATE mineral properties.

LEARN ABOUT how minerals form and how we use them.

LINK to math, writing, social studies, and technology.

◄ A mineral can be different colors. Tourmaline (TOOR•muh•lin) can be pink, purple, green, black, or the mix of colors called watermelon, shown here. Tourmaline is often used in jewelry.

INVESTIGATE

Mineral Properties

Activity Purpose Chalk leaves a mark on a chalkboard because the board is harder than the chalk. Hardness is a property, or characteristic, of minerals, such as the calcite (KAL•syt) that makes up chalk. In this investigation you will **observe** that a mineral can be scratched by some things but not by other things. You will also test other mineral properties and then **classify** minerals by their properties.

Materials

- 6 labeled mineral samples
- hand lens
- streak plate
- copper penny
- steel nail

CAUTION

Activity Procedure

1 Copy the chart shown on page C33.

2 Use the hand lens to **observe** each mineral. Describe the color of each sample. **Record** your observations in the chart. (Picture A)

3 Use each mineral to draw a line across the streak plate. (Picture B) What color is the streak each made? **Record** your observations.

4 **CAUTION** Use caution with the nail, it is sharp. Test the hardness of each mineral by using your fingernail, the copper penny, and the steel nail. Try to scratch each mineral with each of these items. Then try to scratch each sample with each of the other minerals. **Record** your observations in the chart.

Picture A

Picture B

Mineral Sample	Color of the Mineral Sample	Color of the Mineral's Streak	Things That Scratch the Mineral
A			
B			
C			
D			
E			
F			

5 **Classify** the minerals based on each property you tested: color, streak, and hardness. Make labels that list all three properties for each mineral.

Draw Conclusions

1. How are the minerals you tested different from each other?

2. Which of the minerals you tested is the hardest? Explain your choice.

3. **Scientists at Work** Scientists **classify** things so it is easier to study them. How do you think scientists classify minerals?

Investigate Further Obtain five other unknown mineral samples. Determine the hardness, color, and streak of each. **Classify** all of the mineral samples after testing the new samples.

Process Skill Tip

When you **classify** things, you put them into groups based on ways they are alike. Organizing things in this way can make it easier to learn about them. Often, you can classify the same group of objects in many ways.

Diamond Coatings

Perhaps you've seen a ring that holds a diamond— a sparkling natural mineral. But did you know that diamonds can be made? These artificial diamonds aren't made for jewelry but for use by scientists and in factories.

Artificial Diamonds

In nature, diamonds form when carbon is kept at very high pressures and temperatures. It may take millions of years for the diamonds to reach Earth's surface. To make artificial diamonds, scientists imitate the natural process. They use enormous pressures and temperatures to make diamonds in a much shorter time than in nature. However, these diamonds are usually plain-looking and very small. These artificial diamonds have been made since the 1950s.

CVD

Now a new, easier way to make artificial diamonds has been found. It takes high temperature but not high pressure. The new method uses simple hydrocarbons (HY•droh•kar•buhnz). These are materials made of the elements hydrogen and carbon. Scientists heat these materials to very high temperatures. At these temperatures the materials become gases. When the gases cool, they form a thin layer of diamond crystals. This process is called chemical vapor deposition, or CVD. The thin layers of hard diamond crystals are used to protect softer materials.

A thin coating of artificial diamond can protect metal parts. Examples are airplane wings and parts of automobile engines. The coating makes the parts last longer. A thin diamond coating also lowers friction and improves speed. Perhaps someday golf clubs and racing boats will have diamond coatings.

Send Me a Wire

A group of scientists in England is working to develop diamond-coated wires and fibers. The coating adds very little weight but makes the coated materials much stronger. For example, the metal tungsten (TUHNG•stuhn) is too heavy to use as wire for some jobs. But a thin, lightweight wire coated with diamond would work as well as a thicker, heavier, uncoated wire.

Researchers also have removed the wire after it was coated. This leaves behind a very small, hollow diamond tube. These tubes might be used as fiber optic wires for computers, or they could be very fine needles for use by doctors and surgeons.

▶ This microscope photograph shows a diamond crystal growing on a metal surface.

THINK ABOUT IT

1. Why would people want to make artificial diamonds?

2. Why is chemical vapor deposition useful?

CAREERS
ORGANIC CHEMIST

What They Do Organic chemists work with materials containing the element carbon, such as hydrocarbons. These materials include plastics as well as animal and vegetable matter. Organic chemists develop new products or test them. Some organic chemists teach high school or college chemistry

Education and Training Organic chemists have at least a four-year college degree. Most have a master's degree or a Ph.D.

 WEB LINK
For Science and Technology updates, visit the Harcourt Internet site.
www.harcourtschool.com

Mack Gipson, Jr.
STRUCTURAL GEOLOGIST

Mack Gipson grew up on a farm in South Carolina. He helped with farm work and was interested in nature. In junior high, he read a book about Earth and began to wonder how rocks were formed and what caused Earth's layers.

After finishing college with degrees in science and mathematics, Dr. Gipson became a high school teacher. He was drafted into the U.S. Army and trained as a radio technician. While he was with the army in Germany, he decided to go back to school and study geology. He decided he wanted to work outdoors as a geologist rather than spend all day indoors teaching.

One of Dr. Gipson's jobs in college was to test core samples. A core sample shows layers of soil and rock from underground. To get a core sample, a long metal tube is drilled into the ground.

Builders test core samples to make sure the ground can withstand the weight of a building or road. Dr. Gipson tested core samples for the building of runways at O'Hare International Airport in Chicago. He also studied rock layers near coal mines in Illinois.

After graduating from the University of Chicago, Dr. Gipson stayed to help study samples of rock and clay from the ocean floor. This study helped scientists learn about how the oceans have changed over time.

Dr. Gipson founded the Department of Geological Sciences at Virginia State University. In addition to teaching, he has done studies for the National Aeronautics and Space Administration (NASA). He studied pictures of pyramidlike mountains on Mars, concluding that the pictures show extinct volcanoes eroded by the wind.

THINK ABOUT IT

1. How might studying a core sample show how much weight the ground could safely support?

2. What skills do you think are needed to study worlds far from Earth?

Geologists studying core samples

GROWING CRYSTALS

How are minerals left behind by evaporation?

Materials

- plastic gloves
- safety goggles
- apron
- 1 tablespoon of laundry bluing
- 1 tablespoon of water
- 1 tablespoon of ammonia
- 1 tablespoon of table salt
- plastic cup
- spoon
- sponge
- plastic bowl
- food coloring

Procedure

CAUTION Be sure to wear gloves, safety goggles, and an apron.

❶ Mix the bluing, water, ammonia, and salt in the plastic cup. Stir gently until the salt has dissolved.

❷ Place the sponge in the bowl. Pour the mixture over the sponge. Throw away the cup.

❸ Sprinkle 4 drops of food coloring over the sponge. Wait one day.

Draw Conclusions

Observe the sponge. Does it change? What is forming?

WEATHERING ROCK

How can you model weathering by using chalk?

Materials

- 2 pieces of chalk
- plastic jar with lid
- water
- strainer

Procedure

❶ Break each piece of chalk into about three pieces. Put all the chalk pieces except one into the jar.

❷ Pour water into the jar until the chalk is covered. Put the lid on the jar. Make sure it is tightly sealed. Shake the jar for about 5 minutes to "weather" the chalk.

❸ Pour the water through the strainer to get the chalk pieces.

Draw Conclusions

Compare the strained pieces to the chalk that was left out. What happened? Why? Compare this model to real rocks, weathering, and erosion. How are they alike? How are they different?

Vocabulary Review

Use the terms below to complete the sentences. The page numbers in ( ) tell you where to look in the chapter if you need help.

mineral (C36)
streak (C37)
hardness (C37)
luster (C37)
rock (C42)

igneous rock (C42)
sedimentary rock (C44)
metamorphic rock (C46)
rock cycle (C52)

1. A natural, nonliving, solid material that has particles in a repeating pattern is a ____.

2. A ____ is made up of one or more minerals.

3. Limestone is a form of ____.

4. The ____ is the repeating of changes from one kind of rock to another over time.

5. A ____ is a rock changed by heat and pressure.

6. Melted rock cools and hardens to form ____.

7. The color of the powder left behind when you rub a mineral on a white porcelain plate is called the mineral's ____.

8. ____ is a mineral property that describes the way light reflects from the mineral's surface.

9. A mineral's ability to resist being scratched is its ____.

Connect Concepts

Fill in the blanks with the correct terms from the Word Bank.

color   luster   Mohs' hardness scale
hardness   streak

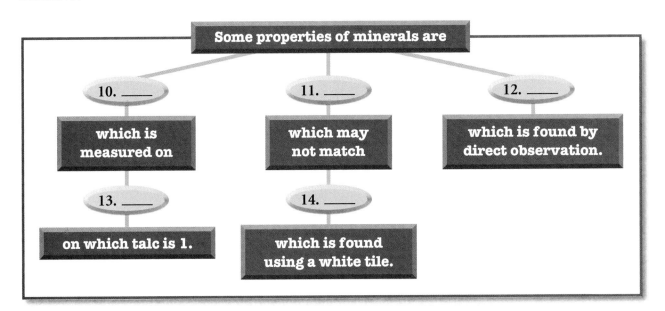

Some properties of minerals are

10. ____ which is measured on

11. ____ which may not match

12. ____ which is found by direct observation.

13. ____ on which talc is 1.

14. ____ which is found using a white tile.

Check Understanding

Write the letter of the best choice.

15. A rock forms in layers of small pieces. It is a ____ rock.
  A sedimentary   **C** igneous
  B mineral   **D** metamorphic

16. Mohs' scale is used to identify a mineral's —
  F color   **H** streak
  G luster   **J** hardness

17. If you describe a mineral as being shiny, you are describing the property of —
  A streak   **C** hardness
  B luster   **D** color

18. A rock that has been changed by pressure and heat is called a(n) ____ rock.
  F sedimentary
  G metamorphic
  H igneous
  J metallic

19. Which of the following minerals is the hardest on Mohs' hardness scale?
  A talc   **C** diamond
  B gypsum   **D** quartz

20. Rocks change over time from one type to another. This process is called —
  F type changing
  G the rock cycle
  H erosion
  J melting

21. Particles in minerals form regular patterns called —
  A crystals   **C** conglomerates
  B layers   **D** shells

Process Skills Review

22. Based on the **model** you made of the rock cycle, what might happen to the "rock" if you made it hot enough to melt?

23. Why do scientists **classify** minerals?

24. How do scientists **classify** rocks?

Critical Thinking

25. How can a metamorphic rock be changed into an igneous rock?

26. Describe the path of a rock through the rock cycle.

Performance Assessment

Mineral Tests

Work with a partner. Use the hand lens to take a closer look at five mineral samples. Make a chart showing all the properties of each mineral. Tell how you tested for each property.

CHAPTER 3

Weather and Climate

Vocabulary Preview

atmosphere
air pressure
humidity
precipitation
evaporation
condensation
local winds
prevailing winds
air mass
front
climate
microclimate
El Niño
greenhouse effect
global warming

Does weather begin or end? Or does it just keep moving from place to place? Many things contribute to making weather and to changing it.

Fast Fact

The United States is a country of many weather extremes. Below are some record-breaking weather measurements.

Heavy Weather

What	Where	How Much
Highest Temperature	Death Valley, CA	134°F
Lowest Temperature	Prospect Creek, AK	⁻79.8°F
Heaviest Snowfall	Mount Shasta, CA	189 in.
Most Snow in a Year	Mount Rainier, WA	1,224.5 in.
Strongest Wind	Mount Washington, NH	231 mi/hr
Most Rain in a Year	Kukui, HI	739 in.

C60

Each summer an average of 6–12 tropical storms form in the Atlantic Ocean, the Caribbean Sea, or the Gulf of Mexico and move toward the United States. If a storm's winds reach 74 miles an hour or more, the storm is called a hurricane.

Fast **Fact**

In 1816 a volcano in Asia blew huge amounts of dust into the atmosphere, blocking some of the sun's rays. That year average temperatures around the world dropped several degrees. In June there were even a few days of snow in the northeastern United States.

C61

How Can You Observe and Measure Weather Conditions?

In this lesson, you can . . .

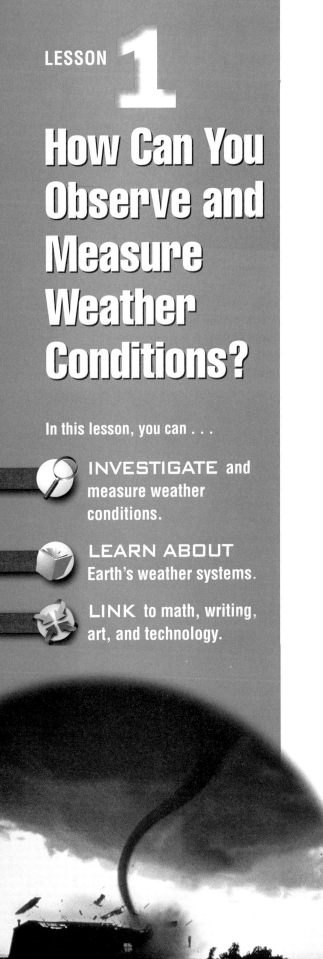

INVESTIGATE and measure weather conditions.

LEARN ABOUT Earth's weather systems.

LINK to math, writing, art, and technology.

INVESTIGATE

Measuring Weather Conditions

Activity Purpose People have always been affected by the weather. But it wasn't until fairly recently that scientists have been able to predict the weather accurately. Today's weather scientists use many instruments to **measure** and **collect data** about weather conditions. Then they use the data to help **predict** what the weather will be like today, tomorrow, or next weekend. In this investigation you will measure and collect data about weather conditions in your area.

Materials
■ weather station

Activity Procedure

1. Make a copy of the Weather Station Daily Record table. You will use it to **record** the date, the time, the temperature, the amount of rain or snow, the wind direction and speed, and the cloud conditions each day for five days. Try to **record** the weather conditions at the same time each day.

2. Place the weather station in a shady spot, 1 m above the ground. **Record** the temperature. (Picture A)

3. Be sure the rain gauge will not collect runoff from any buildings or trees. **Record** the amount of rain or snow (if any).

◀ A Midwest tornado

Weather Station Daily Record

Date				
Time				
Temperature				
Rainfall or snowfall				
Wind direction and speed				
Cloud conditions				

Picture A

4 Be sure the wind vane is located where wind from any direction will reach it. **Record** the wind direction and speed. Winds are labeled with the direction from which they blow. (Picture B)

5 Describe and **record** the cloud conditions by noting how much of the sky is covered by clouds. Draw a circle and shade in the part of the circle that equals the amount of sky covered with clouds.

6 Use the temperature data to make a line graph showing how the temperature changes from day to day.

Picture B

Draw Conclusions

1. Use your Weather Station Daily Record to **compare** the weather conditions on two different days. Which conditions were about the same? Which conditions changed the most?

2. From the **data** you **gathered** in this activity, how might scientists use weather data to **predict** the weather?

3. **Scientists at Work** Scientists learn about the weather by **measuring** weather conditions and **gathering data.** What did you learn by measuring the amount of rain your area received during the week of your observations?

Investigate Further Find a newspaper weather page, and note the temperatures in various cities throughout the United States. **Hypothesize** why there are different temperatures in different cities. **Plan and conduct a simple investigation** to find out.

Process Skill Tip

Measurements are a kind of observation. You **measure** when you use a tool, such as a thermometer or rain gauge, to **gather data** about something.

Weather Systems

Where Weather Occurs

FIND OUT

- where most weather occurs
- how weather conditions are measured
- how clouds form

VOCABULARY

atmosphere
air pressure
humidity
precipitation
evaporation
condensation

Almost all weather occurs in the lowest layer of air, or **atmosphere**, that surrounds Earth. The atmosphere stretches about 1000 km (620 mi) from the Earth's surface to outer space. The lowest layer of the atmosphere, called the *troposphere*, is where most water is found and where most clouds form. The troposphere is about 15 km (9 mi) thick at the equator.

Very little weather occurs above the troposphere. There is a little water in the *stratosphere,* the next higher layer, so a few clouds form there. But more important is the stratosphere's ozone layer, about 22.5 km (14 mi) above the Earth's surface. Ozone protects life on Earth by absorbing some of the sun's harmful rays. From the stratosphere to the edge of space, there is no water and too little air for any weather to occur.

✔ **In what layer of the atmosphere does most of Earth's weather occur?**

Blizzards, at the left, and hurricanes, at the right, are among the largest and most powerful weather systems of Earth's troposphere, shown below.

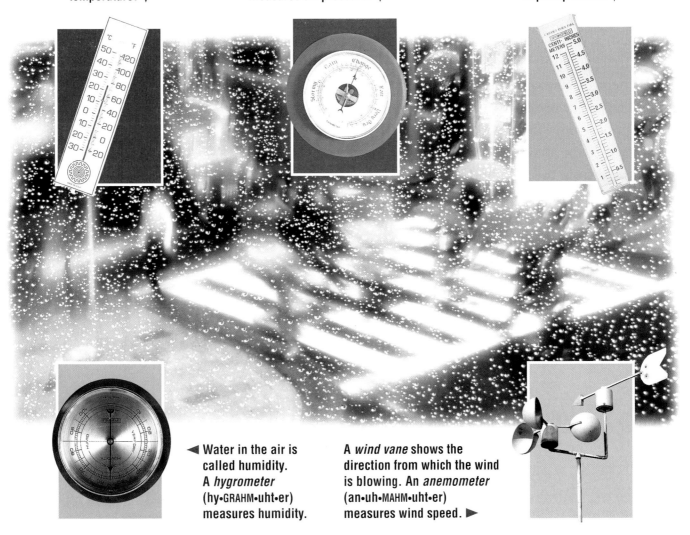

A *thermometer* measures air temperature. ▼

Air pressure is the weight of the atmosphere. A *barometer* measures air pressure. ▼

A *rain gauge* measures the amount of precipitation. ▼

◄ Water in the air is called humidity. A *hygrometer* (hy•GRAHM•uht•er) measures humidity.

A *wind vane* shows the direction from which the wind is blowing. An *anemometer* (an•uh•MAHM•uht•er) measures wind speed. ►

Measuring Atmospheric Conditions

The weather changes because the atmosphere is constantly changing. Sometimes the air is cold and sometimes it's warm. As air warms, its weight, or **air pressure**, lessens. And warm air holds more water, or can have more **humidity**, than cold air. These and other conditions of the atmosphere can be observed and measured.

The weather instruments shown on this page can be used to measure atmospheric conditions—air temperature, air pressure, **precipitation** (rain or snow), humidity, wind direction, and wind speed. Other atmospheric conditions, such as cloud type, are observed directly.

Why do people measure atmospheric conditions? One reason is to predict what the weather will be. For example, a change in air pressure or cloud type often means there will be a change in the weather.

✔ **What are some atmospheric conditions that can be measured?**

Air Pressure

You probably don't feel the atmosphere weighing you down. But air does have weight. The atmosphere pushes on you all the time, and this weight is air pressure.

There are several types of barometers for measuring air pressure. A mercury barometer, like the ones shown at the right, consists of a glass tube about 1 m (3 ft) long. Air is removed from the tube, and the glass is sealed at the top. Then the tube is turned upside down, and the open end is placed in a dish of mercury. The weight of the air pushing down on the mercury in the dish pushes mercury up into the glass tube. The mercury rises in the tube until its weight exactly balances the weight of the air pushing down on the mercury in the dish. The height of the mercury in the tube is a measure of air pressure. This measure is compared to a standard, or average, air pressure of about 76 cm (30 in.) of mercury.

Recall that warm air weighs less than cold air. A mass of cold air, called a *high-pressure area,* will measure more than 76 cm of mercury. A mass of warm air, called a *low-pressure area,* will measure less than 76 cm of mercury.

Weather changes because high- and low-pressure areas move. In the winter, areas of high pressure often move from northwestern Canada toward the southeastern United States, bringing cool, dry weather conditions. In the summer, areas of low pressure often move from the Gulf of Mexico to the northeastern United States, bringing warm, wet weather conditions.

As these high-pressure and low-pressure areas move, barometer readings in their paths change. Therefore, changing

HIGH AIR PRESSURE

The mercury in this barometer is high. Areas of high pressure usually have fair weather.

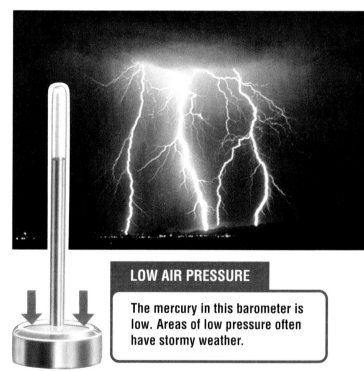

LOW AIR PRESSURE

The mercury in this barometer is low. Areas of low pressure often have stormy weather.

barometer readings can be used to predict changes in weather. If the barometer is rising, the weather will probably become fair. If the barometer is falling, stormy weather is probably coming.

✔ **How can changing air pressure be used to predict changing weather conditions?**

Water in the Air

In addition to temperature and air pressure, humidity, or the amount of water in the air, is an important factor in describing weather conditions. But how does water get into the air?

Earth's oceans are the biggest source of water. As the sun heats the oceans, liquid water changes into an invisible gas called *water vapor,* which rises into the air. The process of liquid water changing to water vapor is called **evaporation**. High up in the atmosphere, where the air is cooler, water vapor turns back into liquid drops of water, forming clouds. This process is called **condensation**.

When cloud drops come together, gravity returns the water to the Earth's surface as precipitation—usually rain. If the temperature in the clouds is below freezing, the precipitation is sleet, hail, or snow. This transferring of water from the Earth's surface to the atmosphere and back is called *water cycle.*

THE INSIDE STORY

The Water Cycle

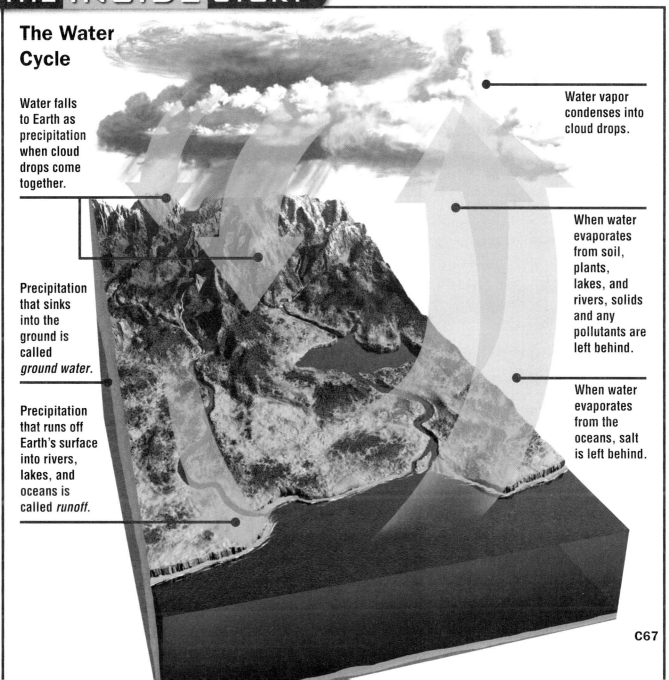

Water falls to Earth as precipitation when cloud drops come together.

Precipitation that sinks into the ground is called *ground water.*

Precipitation that runs off Earth's surface into rivers, lakes, and oceans is called *runoff.*

Water vapor condenses into cloud drops.

When water evaporates from soil, plants, lakes, and rivers, solids and any pollutants are left behind.

When water evaporates from the oceans, salt is left behind.

On clear nights, when the surface of the Earth cools quickly, water vapor may condense to form a cloud near the ground. This low cloud is called *fog*. If you have ever walked through fog, you know what the inside of a cloud is like.

Whether a cloud forms near the ground or high in the atmosphere, it forms in the same way. Water vapor condenses onto dust and other tiny particles in the air when it rises and cools. Another way in which air cools enough for water vapor to condense is by moving from a warm place to a colder place. For example, moist air that moves from over a warm body of water to over cooler land forms clouds or fog.

Even though all clouds form by condensation, different weather conditions produce different types of clouds. Weather scientists, or *meteorologists* (meet•ee•uhr•AHL•uh•juhsts),

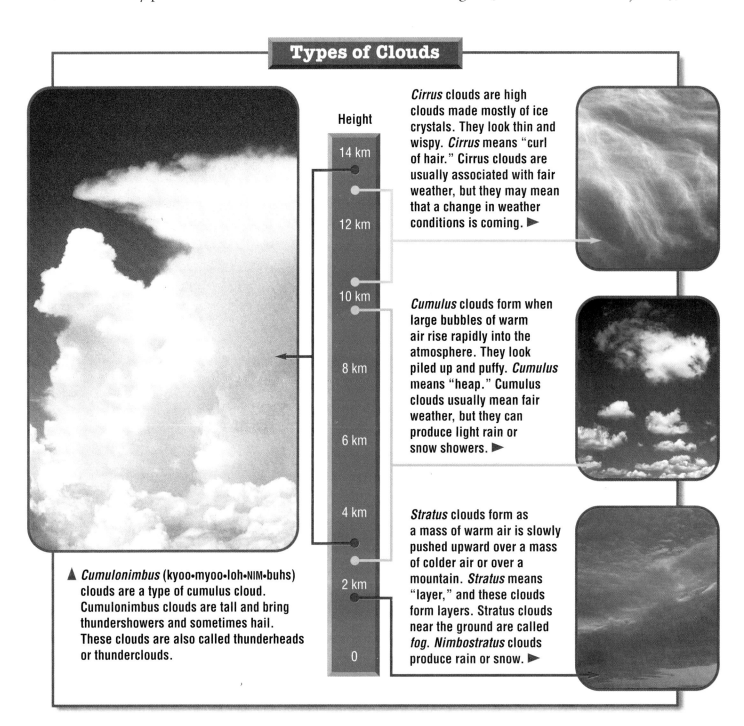

Types of Clouds

Height

14 km
12 km
10 km
8 km
6 km
4 km
2 km
0

Cirrus clouds are high clouds made mostly of ice crystals. They look thin and wispy. *Cirrus* means "curl of hair." Cirrus clouds are usually associated with fair weather, but they may mean that a change in weather conditions is coming. ▶

Cumulus clouds form when large bubbles of warm air rise rapidly into the atmosphere. They look piled up and puffy. *Cumulus* means "heap." Cumulus clouds usually mean fair weather, but they can produce light rain or snow showers. ▶

Stratus clouds form as a mass of warm air is slowly pushed upward over a mass of colder air or over a mountain. *Stratus* means "layer," and these clouds form layers. Stratus clouds near the ground are called *fog*. *Nimbostratus* clouds produce rain or snow. ▶

▲ *Cumulonimbus* (kyoo•myoo•loh•NIM•buhs) clouds are a type of cumulus cloud. Cumulonimbus clouds are tall and bring thundershowers and sometimes hail. These clouds are also called thunderheads or thunderclouds.

give clouds three basic names—cirrus (SEER•uhs), cumulus (KYOO•myoo•luhs), and stratus. Along with other information, the types of clouds in the atmosphere can be used to help predict weather changes. Some basic types of clouds and their descriptions are shown on page C68.

✔ **How do clouds form?**

Summary

Most of Earth's weather takes place in the troposphere, the lowest layer of the atmosphere. Weather conditions such as temperature, air pressure, humidity, wind speed and direction, and the amount of precipitation can be observed and measured. Certain weather conditions, such as changing air pressure and types of clouds, can be used to predict changes in the weather.

Review

1. How do weather scientists **observe** and **measure** weather conditions?
2. How is water recycled in the water cycle?
3. What causes clouds to form?
4. **Critical Thinking** It is a gray, cloudy day, and a light rain is falling. What type of clouds would you expect to see? Explain your answer.
5. **Test Prep** The process by which water vapor turns into liquid water drops is known as —

   A condensation
   B evaporation
   C precipitation
   D the water cycle

LINKS

MATH LINK

Multiply/Divide Decimals Many meteorologists in the United States measure air pressure in units called *millibars*. At sea level, standard air pressure is 1013.2 millibars. If 1013.2 millibars equals 76 cm of mercury, what would a barometer reading of 75 cm of mercury equal in millibars?

WRITING LINK

Informative Writing—Report Suppose that you are a meteorologist who has just spotted a large cumulonimbus cloud moving toward a city. Write a weather report for the city's residents.

ART LINK

Stormy Weather Make a drawing that includes one or more of the cloud types shown on page C68. Show the weather conditions that are associated with those cloud types.

GO **TECHNOLOGY LINK**
ONLINE

Learn more about Earth's atmosphere by visiting the Harcourt Learning Site.
www.harcourtschool.com

WELCOME TO
THE
LEARNING
SITE

What Causes Weather?

In this lesson, you can . . .

 INVESTIGATE the rates at which water and soil absorb and release heat.

 LEARN ABOUT uneven heating of the Earth's surface and the movement of air masses as the causes of weather.

 LINK to math, writing, music, and technology.

◀ Energy to fly this kite starts with the sun.

 **INVESTIGATE**

The Sun's Energy Heats Unevenly

Activity Purpose If you've ever walked barefoot from pavement to grass on a sunny day, you know that different materials absorb heat differently. On a larger scale, uneven heating like this is what produces wind. In this investigation you will **predict** which material heats up and cools off faster—water or soil. Then you will test your predictions.

Materials

- 2 tin cans (lids removed)
- water
- dry soil
- spoon
- 2 thermometers

Activity Procedure

1 Fill one can about $\frac{3}{4}$ full of water and the other can about $\frac{3}{4}$ full of soil. (Picture A)

2 Place one thermometer in the can of water and the other in the can of soil. Put the cans in a shady place outside. Wait for 10 minutes, and then **record** the temperatures of the water and the soil.

3 Put both cans in sunlight. **Predict** which of the cans will show the faster rise in temperature. **Record** the temperature of each can every 10 minutes for 30 minutes. In which can does the temperature rise faster? Which material—soil or water—heats up faster? (Picture B)

Picture A

4. Now put the cans back in the shade. **Predict** in which of the cans the temperature will drop faster. Again **record** the temperature of each can every 10 minutes for 30 minutes. In which can does the temperature drop faster? Which material—soil or water—cools off faster?

5. Make line graphs to show how the temperatures of both materials changed as they heated up and cooled off.

Picture B

Draw Conclusions

1. How did your results match your predictions? Which material—water or soil—heated up faster? Which cooled off faster?

2. From the results you **observed** in this investigation, which would you **predict** heats up faster—oceans or land? Which would you predict cools off faster? Explain.

3. **Scientists at Work** Scientists learn by **predicting** and then testing their predictions. How did you test your predictions about water and soil?

Investigate Further **Hypothesize** how fast materials, such as moist soil, sand, or salt water, heat up and cool off. **Plan and conduct a simple experiment** to test your hypothesis.

> **Process Skill Tip**
>
> A prediction is based on previous observations. Before you **predict**, think about what you have already observed.

What Is Climate and How Does It Change?

In this lesson, you can . . .

INVESTIGATE local weather conditions.

LEARN ABOUT climates and how they change.

LINK to math, writing, literature, and technology.

INVESTIGATE

Local Weather Conditions

Activity Purpose Why does the temperature change as you go from the city to the country? Why is a city park cooler than nearby streets and sidewalks? You know that different parts of the country often have different weather conditions. In this investigation you'll find out if places very close to each other can have different weather conditions, too.

Materials

- 4 metersticks
- 4 weather stations

Activity Procedure

1. Make a table like the one shown on page C79.

2. Choose four locations near your school to study. Select different kinds of locations, such as a shady parkway, a sunny playground, a parking lot on the south side of your school, and a ball field on the north side. For the same time on any given day, **predict** whether the temperature, wind direction, and wind speed will be the same or different at the different locations.

3. At the chosen time, four people should each take a meterstick and a weather station to a different one of the selected locations. Use the meterstick to locate a point 1 m above the ground. **Measure** and **record** the temperature at that point. Use the weather station to determine the wind direction and speed, too. Record the data in your table. (Pictures A and B)

Picture A

Picture B

4 Make a double-bar graph to show the temperatures and wind speeds recorded at all the locations. Write the wind direction at each location on the appropriate wind-speed bar.

Local Weather Conditions

	1	2	3	4
Location				
Temperature				
Wind Direction				
Wind Speed				

Draw Conclusions

1. Use your table to **compare** the temperature, wind direction, and wind speed at the different locations. What differences, if any, did you find? What conditions were the same?

2. Local weather conditions affect the organisms that live in a location. Do you think wind speed or temperature is more likely to affect living organisms? Explain.

3. Based on your investigation, how would you define the phrase *local weather conditions*?

4. **Scientists at Work** Scientists learn about local weather conditions by **comparing** weather data from different locations. **Draw conclusions** about local weather conditions, based on the locations you studied.

Investigate Further What other factors, in addition to temperature, wind direction, and wind speed, might affect local weather conditions? **Hypothesize** about a factor that might affect local weather conditions. Then **plan and conduct a simple experiment** to test your hypothesis.

Process Skill Tip

You **compare** before you **draw conclusions** about what is the same and what is different about weather conditions in different locations.

C79

Jacob Bjerknes discovered the warm current, called El Niño, that sometimes produces severe weather along the Pacific coast.

Major Events in Weather Forecasting

FIN
• w
  cl
• h
  ca

V
cl
m
El
g
gl

At the
you v
clima
anim

The History of Weather Forecasting

350 B.C.
Aristotle writes *Meteorologica*, a book about weather observations.

1835
Coriolis discovers what is later called the "Coriolis Effect."

1902
Scientists discover that the atmosphere has layers. The troposphere and stratosphere are identified.

| 400 B.C. | A.D. 1600 | A.D. 1700 | A.D. 1800 |

1600
Early weather instruments are invented.

1849
The first weather report sent by telegraph is received by Joseph Henry, secretary of the Smithsonian Institution.

1890
Congress forms an agency called the Weather Bureau, later renamed the National Weather Service.

In ancient times, weather predictions were based on superstitions. It seemed to make sense that good weather depended on the happiness of the gods. Yet as early as the year 100, Egyptian scientists showed that air expanded when it was heated. This early discovery led to other advances in meteorology, the study of weather.

Observing Weather Systems

In 1735 scientists observed that the sun heated areas near the equator more strongly than areas north or south of the equator. They also discovered that as air above the equator expands, it moves toward the cooler latitudes. This movement results in a global wind pattern, which causes a global weather pattern.

This discovery was followed by the discovery of the "trade winds" north and south of the equator and other wind zones in the Northern Hemisphere. In 1835 French physicist Gustave Coriolis described the movement of air masses north and south of the equator. He showed how winds north or south of the equator curve in different directions. Coriolis realized that these curved air routes were caused by the rotation of Earth.

Modern Forecasting

Wind vanes had long been used to determine wind direction, but it wasn't until the 1600s that instruments were invented that could accurately measure other weather conditions. In 1644 the first barometer was made. In 1754 G. D. Fahrenheit made the first mercury thermometer.

At least 100 years ago, scientists knew that they could improve their forecasts if they had measurements from enough weather stations around the world. Today there are tens of thousands of weather stations. Each station takes many measurements—temperature, humidity, cloud cover, wind speed and direction, and barometric pressure. Modern communication systems allow scientists to share this information almost instantly. This allows warnings to be issued to people who might be affected by severe weather events.

Weather satellites, first launched in the 1960s, provide the most important data for modern weather forecasting. Satellite data helps scientists understand the global forces that cause local weather conditions. Today countries around the world share satellite weather data.

THINK ABOUT IT

1. What causes winds to curve?
2. What is the most important instrument for weather forecasters today? Explain.

1950s
Bjerknes makes the connection between the El Niño current and certain reversed weather patterns.

1980s
Doppler radar is first used.

A.D. 1900   A.D. 2000

1960s
The first weather satellites are launched.

1990s
International cooperation and the use of satellites increases understanding of worldwide weather patterns.

NIMBUS SPACECRAFT

Carolyn Kloth

METEOROLOGIST

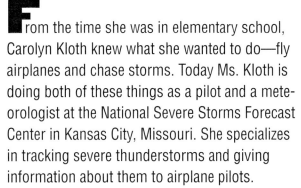

"A lot of people tend to think that you need to be able to look out of a window to assess the weather. With the use of radar, weather satellites, and all of the other weather data available, you can do the job almost anywhere."

From the time she was in elementary school, Carolyn Kloth knew what she wanted to do—fly airplanes and chase storms. Today Ms. Kloth is doing both of these things as a pilot and a meteorologist at the National Severe Storms Forecast Center in Kansas City, Missouri. She specializes in tracking severe thunderstorms and giving information about them to airplane pilots.

At the severe storms center, Ms. Kloth receives weather data every hour from across North America. The data includes images of cloud patterns, locations of fronts, and the number of lightning strikes. She also studies measurements of air pressure, humidity, precipitation, and temperature, both at the ground and at various levels in the atmosphere. Once all the data has come in, Ms. Kloth uses computers to analyze it. Then she predicts where severe thunderstorms are likely to form across the continent and over nearby coastal waters.

Ms. Kloth issues severe storm warnings to pilots for any storm that has winds of more than 26 m/s, hail larger than 19 mm in diameter, or clouds that may form tornadoes. She finds that about 1 percent of all thunderstorms fit into one or more of those categories. The warnings that Ms. Kloth issues help pilots avoid thunderstorms and result in safer and more comfortable flights.

THINK ABOUT IT

1. How can Ms. Kloth gather weather data without looking out a window?
2. How do you think Ms. Kloth's experience as a pilot helps her in her job at the National Severe Storms Forecast Center?

AIR PRESSURE

How strong is air pressure?

Materials

- plastic sandwich bag
- drinking straw
- tape
- heavy book

Procedure

❶ Put one end of the straw in the plastic bag. Then seal the bag shut with tape.

❷ Put the plastic bag on a table and lay the book on part of the bag as shown.

❸ Blow through the straw into the bag, and observe what happens.

Draw Conclusions

Describe what happened to the bag and the book. Explain what happened. Try to think of a situation where air pressure could be used like this.

SIDEWALK GRAPH

How does sunlight speed up evaporation?

Materials

- sunny sidewalk
- 500 mL water
- chalk
- clock

Procedure

❶ Pour about 500 mL of water onto a sidewalk that is in full sunlight.

❷ Draw a line around the outside of the puddle with the chalk.

❸ Draw a new line around the puddle every 5 min for 20 min.

❹ Repeat the experiment on a sidewalk in the shade.

Draw Conclusions

Compare the sizes of the puddles at each 5-min interval. Based on your observations, predict how long it would take for each puddle to evaporate.

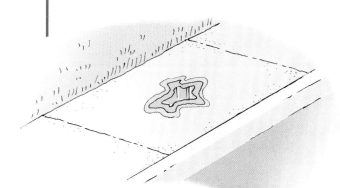

Vocabulary Review

Use the terms below to complete the sentences. The page numbers in ( ) tell you where to look in the chapter if you need help.

atmosphere (C64)   **air mass** (C75)

air pressure (C65)   **front** (C75)

humidity (C65)   **climate** (C80)

precipitation (C65)   **microclimate** (C80)

evaporation (C67)   **El Niño** (C83)

condensation (C67)   **greenhouse effect** (C84)

local winds (C73)   **global warming** (C84)

prevailing winds (C73)

1. Liquid water changes to water vapor through the process of ____. Water vapor turns back into liquid drops of water through the process of ____.

2. Almost all weather occurs in the lowest layer of the ____.

3. Rain or snow is called ____.

4. Water in the air is called ____.

5. The weight of air is known as ____.

6. Global winds that blow constantly from the same direction are known as ____.

7. Winds that depend on local changes in temperature are called ____.

8. The climate of a small area is called a ____.

9. The boundary between air masses is called a ____.

10. The average of an area's weather conditions through all seasons over a period of time is called ____.

11. Excess carbon dioxide in the atmosphere may lead to ____.

12. The process by which carbon dioxide in the atmosphere absorbs some of the heat given off by Earth is called the ____.

13. One example of a short-term climate change is ____.

14. A body of air with nearly the same temperature and humidity throughout is an ____.

Connect Concepts

Copy and complete the idea clusters below, which describe weather and climate.

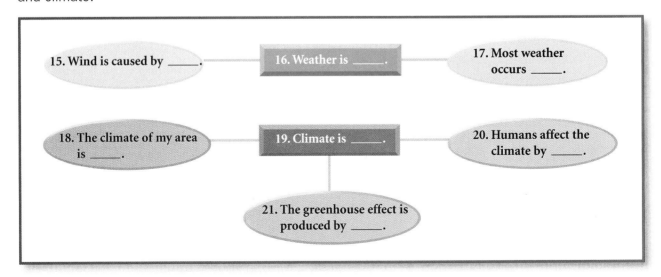

15. Wind is caused by ____.

16. Weather is ____.

17. Most weather occurs ____.

18. The climate of my area is ____.

19. Climate is ____.

20. Humans affect the climate by ____.

21. The greenhouse effect is produced by ____.

Check Understanding

Write the letter of the best choice.

22. As air warms, —
    A air pressure increases
    B air pressure decreases
    C temperature decreases
    D humidity changes

23. A wind vane indicates —
    F air pressure   H humidity
    G wind speed   J wind direction

24. Wind is caused when air —
    A moves from the land to the sea
    B moves from the sea to the land
    C moves from an area of higher
      pressure to an area of lower pressure
    D moves from an area of lower pressure
      to an area of higher pressure

25. Prevailing winds are caused by the
    uneven heating of Earth's atmosphere
    and by —
    F local winds   H Earth's rotation
    G air pressure   J temperature

26. Florida has a warmer climate than
    Maine because Florida —
    A is closer to the South Pole
    B is closer to the equator
    C is nearer to the Atlantic Ocean
    D receives more precipitation

27. Most of the eastern United States and
    the West Coast have a climate that is —
    F mountain   H desert
    G polar   J temperate

Critical Thinking

28. How does the location of Hawai'i, near
    the equator, affect its climate?

29. Suppose you live in the middle of the
    United States and are looking at a
    weather map. To the north and east of
    your location, it is warm and raining. To
    the west and south, the weather is cold
    and clear. What sort of weather can you
    expect before tomorrow? Explain.

Process Skills Review

30. A thermometer measures air tempera-
    ture. A barometer measures air pressure.
    A hygrometer measures humidity, and a
    rain gauge measures precipitation.
    Which two of these instruments are
    most useful for the **measurements** that
    determine a region's climate? Explain.

31. Which would you **predict** would heat
    up faster on a sunny day—a pond or a
    meadow? Explain.

32. **Compare** weather and climate.

Performance Assessment

Your Weather and Climate

Look at a map of the United States.
Explain where weather in your area comes
from. Describe any local conditions that
affect the weather. Then identify the climate
zone in which you are
located—polar, tropi-
cal, temperate,
desert, or mountain.
Explain what
determines
your climate
zone.

Exploring the Oceans

Vocabulary Preview

salinity
water pressure
wave
current
tide
shore
headland
tide pool
jetty
scuba
submersible
sonar
desalination

If you've ever been to the beach, it may have seemed to you that the water always moves toward the shore. But the movement of ocean water is more complex than that. In addition to causing waves, winds make ocean waters move in great loops around the world.

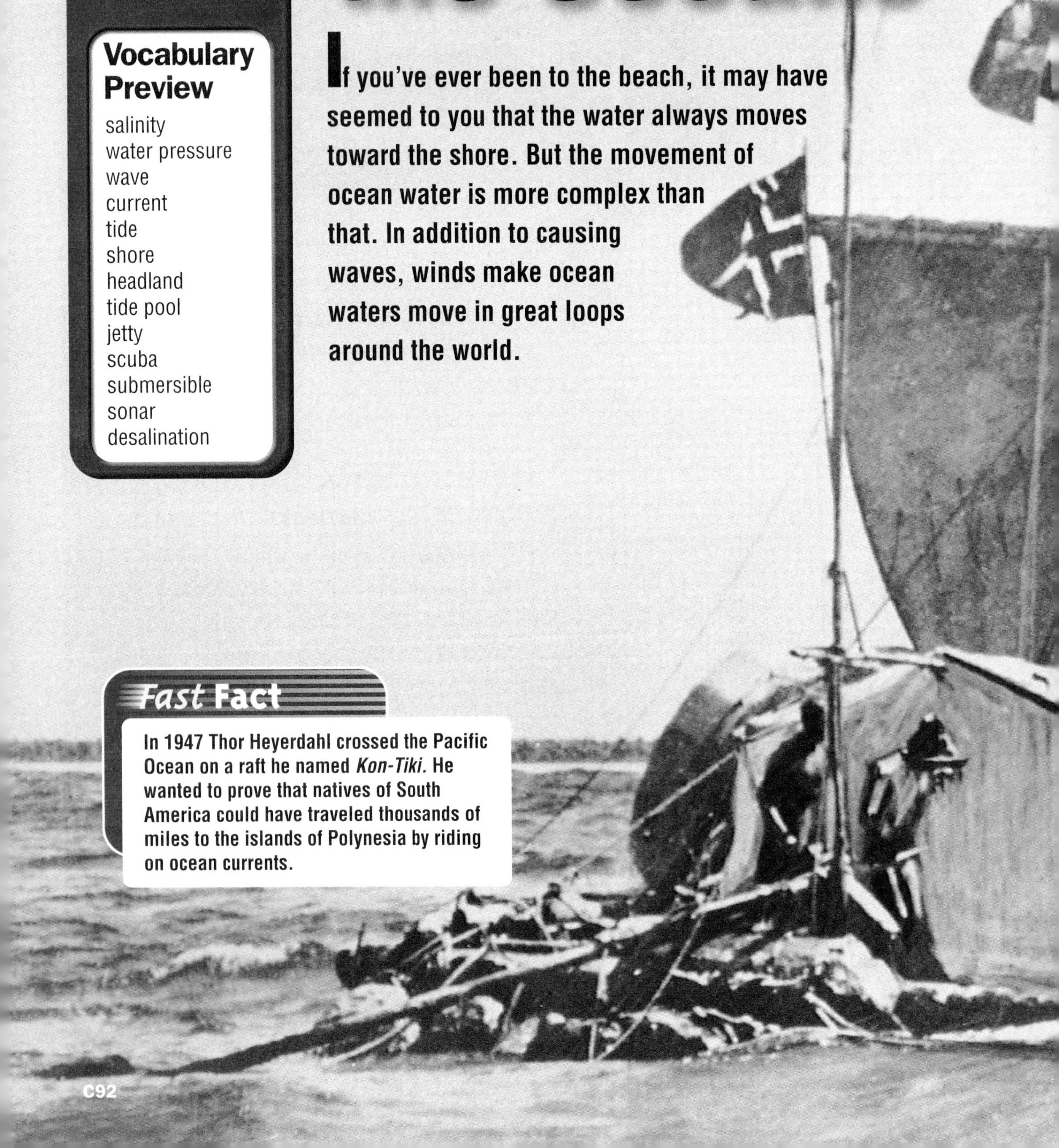

Fast Fact

In 1947 Thor Heyerdahl crossed the Pacific Ocean on a raft he named *Kon-Tiki*. He wanted to prove that natives of South America could have traveled thousands of miles to the islands of Polynesia by riding on ocean currents.

Fast Fact

If a bay and a river that empties into it are narrow and shallow, high tides can move rapidly upriver. A wall of water, called a *tidal bore,* forms at the front of the tide.

Fast Fact

The deepest spot in Earth's oceans is the Mariana Trench, in the western Pacific. It is 11,033 m (36,198 ft) deep, and was explored in 1960 by the submersible *Trieste III,* shown here. Mount Everest, the highest mountain, is only 8848 m (29,028 ft) high.

Average Ocean Depths

Ocean	Depth (meters)
Pacific	4188
Indian	3872
Atlantic	3735
Arctic	1038

1

What Are the Oceans Like?

In this lesson, you can . . .

 INVESTIGATE how salt affects the freezing temperature of water.

 LEARN ABOUT oceans and seas, ocean water, and the ocean floor.

 LINK to math, writing, social studies, and technology.

Icebreakers help keep shipping lanes open in the frozen waters of the Arctic Ocean. ▼

INVESTIGATE

Icy Water

Activity Purpose   Have you ever skated on a frozen pond? In cold places, freshwater ponds and lakes often freeze in winter. Even in the coldest weather, however, ocean water rarely freezes, except in the very cold Arctic and Antarctic regions. In this activity you will **compare** the temperatures of icy fresh water and salt water. Then you will **predict** the temperature at which salt water will freeze.

Materials

- 2 plastic measuring cups
- wax pencil
- ice cubes
- water
- spoon
- salt
- thermometer

Activity Procedure

1 Make a copy of the chart shown below. You will use it to **record data** you collect.

Water Temperatures

Cup A		Cup B	
Spoonfuls of Salt	Temp.	Spoonfuls of Salt	Temp.
0		0	
0		2	
0		4	
0		6	

2 Use the wax pencil to label the cups A and B. Fill each cup with ice cubes. Then add equal amounts of water to each cup.

3 Wait 5 minutes, and then use the thermometer to **measure** the temperature of the water in each cup. Record the temperatures in the chart. (Picture A)

4 Stir two heaping spoonfuls of salt into cup B. (Picture B)

5 Wait 2 minutes, and then measure the temperature of the water in each cup again. Record these temperatures in the chart.

6 Repeat Steps 4 and 5 two more times. Each time, stir to dissolve the salt in cup B, and then measure and record the temperature of the water in each cup.

Picture A

Picture B

Draw Conclusions

1. **Compare** the final temperatures of the two cups of water. What happened to the temperature of the salt water as more salt was added to cup B?

2. Based on your results, **predict** the temperature at which the water in cup B would freeze.

3. **Scientists at Work** The Arctic Ocean tends to be less salty, on average, than the Atlantic Ocean. Scientists use this information to predict when winter temperatures will cause certain harbors and ports to freeze. Explain why cold winter temperatures would affect the formation of harbor ice differently in the two oceans.

Investigate Further **Hypothesize** how the amount of salt in water affects the temperature at which the water will freeze. Then **plan and conduct a simple experiment** using varying amounts of salt dissolved in water to test your hypothesis.

Process Skill Tip

When you **compare** data, you note what is similar or different about two sets of data. After comparing data, you can **predict** what might happen in similar situations.

Earth's Oceans

Oceans and Seas

Nearly 71 percent of Earth's surface is covered with a continuous body of salty water. Geographers have divided this body into four oceans and many smaller seas. As you can see from the table below, the Pacific Ocean is the largest ocean. It is equal in size to the other three oceans combined. It is also the deepest ocean, with an average depth of 4188 m (about 13,740 ft). The Atlantic Ocean is shallower, with an average depth of only 3735 m (about 12,254 ft). Much of the surface of the Arctic Ocean, the smallest ocean, is covered with ice all year round. In ocean areas near Antarctica, the surface water freezes for at least part of the year.

Seas are smaller than oceans. Seas may be partly surrounded by land or separated from an ocean by a chain of islands. Some bodies of water, such as the Gulf of Mexico, are really seas, even though they have a different name.

✔ **Name Earth's four large oceans.**

Earth's Oceans	
Name	**Surface Area** (in millions of km²)
Pacific Ocean	166.0
Atlantic Ocean	82.4
Indian Ocean	74.0
Arctic Ocean	14.1

More than 70 percent of Earth's surface is covered by oceans and seas. ▼

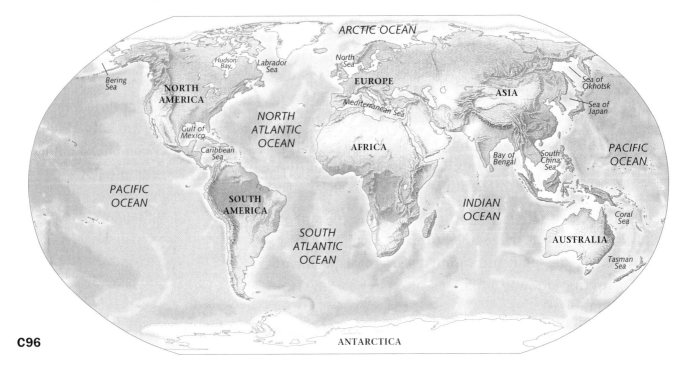

Characteristics of Ocean Water

The most obvious characteristic of ocean water is its **salinity**, or saltiness. The world's oceans and seas taste salty because of minerals dissolved in the water. The main mineral in ocean water is sodium chloride—ordinary table salt.

In addition to sodium chloride, ocean water has other minerals and gases dissolved in it. Many of the minerals in ocean water come from the weathering of rocks on land.

The salinity of ocean water varies from place to place. In warm, dry regions, evaporation of water from the ocean surface and little precipitation cause ocean water to have a high salinity. In cold regions, salinity is lower because less evaporation takes place and melting ice and snow add fresh water. Areas of lower salinity also occur where freshwater rivers enter the ocean.

Extreme pressure is another characteristic of ocean water. On land, air pressure is about

On Bonaire, an island in the Caribbean Sea near Venezuela, many evaporation ponds have been built for the collection of sea salts. After the water evaporates, salt is left behind.

14.7 lb per sq in. This amount of pressure is referred to as one atmosphere. Water weighs more than air. In the ocean, with each additional 10 m (about 33 ft) of depth, **water pressure**—the weight of the water pressing on an object—increases by one atmosphere. In the deepest parts of the oceans, water pressure can be as high as 1000 atmospheres. Exploration at these depths requires special equipment such as the bathyscaphe *Trieste* shown below.

✔ **What are some causes of high salinity in ocean water?**

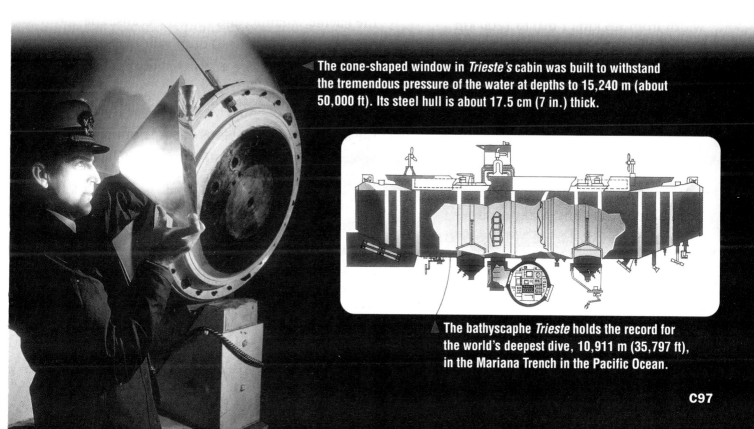

The cone-shaped window in *Trieste's* cabin was built to withstand the tremendous pressure of the water at depths to 15,240 m (about 50,000 ft). Its steel hull is about 17.5 cm (7 in.) thick.

The bathyscaphe *Trieste* holds the record for the world's deepest dive, 10,911 m (35,797 ft), in the Mariana Trench in the Pacific Ocean.

How Do Ocean Waters Move?

In this lesson, you can . . .

INVESTIGATE waves.

LEARN ABOUT the movement of ocean waters.

LINK to math, writing, language arts, and technology.

INVESTIGATE

Waves

Activity Purpose Have you ever stood on a beach and watched the ocean? If so, you probably noticed that the water is always moving in waves. Waves can also move across a lake or a pond. You can even **observe** very small waves, called ripples, on a puddle. What causes waves? In the investigation, you will **use a model** of the ocean to find out.

Materials

- rectangular pan
- water
- straw

Activity Procedure

1 **Make a model** of the ocean by half-filling the pan with water. (Picture A)

2 Place your straw near one side of the pan, and gently blow across the surface of the water. What happens? (Picture B)

◄ Wind and waves work together to make windsurfing an exciting sport.

Picture A

Picture B

3 **Observe** the height and speed of the waves you make. **Record** your observations.

4 Repeat Step 2 several times, blowing a little harder each time. What do you **observe** about the waves you make? **Record** your observations.

Draw Conclusions

1. Use your observations to describe the relationship between how hard you blow and the height and speed of the waves.

2. From what you observed in this activity, what can you **infer** about the cause of waves on oceans and other bodies of water?

3. **Scientists at Work** Scientists often **use models** to learn about things they cannot **observe** directly. What did your model help you observe about waves?

Investigate Further **Hypothesize** how high the waves on a pond, a lake, or the ocean can be on a calm day or on a stormy day. Then **plan and conduct a simple experiment** to test your hypothesis.

Process Skill Tip

Observing is the most basic science skill. You **observe** when you use your senses to note the properties of an object or event, such as the effect of moving air on water.

How Ocean Waters Move

Wind and Waves

The waters of the ocean never stop moving. Most of the movement of water on the ocean's surface is due to waves. A **wave** is the up-and-down movement of surface water.

In the investigation you observed that wind produces waves. In fact, most waves are caused by wind. When wind blows over the surface of a body of water, it causes the surface of the water to move with it. Because water moves more slowly than air, the water piles up, forming a ripple. The wind then pushes on the side of the ripple, making it grow in height, and turning the ripple into a wave.

In the investigation you also observed that the height of a wave is related to how hard the wind blows. On a calm day, ocean waves may be less than 1.5 m (about 5 ft) high. But during a storm, waves can reach heights of 30 m (about 100 ft). That's as high as a ten-story building!

Even though the water in a wave may rise and fall by as much as 30 m, very little of the water moves forward. What moves across the ocean's surface is energy. Think about this: When you shake a rope, the rope moves up and down or side to side as waves travel to the

Water in a wave moves in circles, returning to about the place where it started. ▼

end of the rope. But the rope itself doesn't move forward. This motion is similar to what happens to water in the ocean. The waves move across the surface of the water, but the water stays in almost the same place.

✔ **What causes most waves in water?**

Other Kinds of Waves

Most ocean waves are caused by wind. But some waves can be caused by earthquakes and volcanoes, extremely low air pressure, or several things acting together.

Some of the biggest waves in the oceans are caused by earthquakes and volcanoes. These giant waves are called *tsunamis* (soo•NAH•meez). In the deep ocean, a tsunami may be more than 100 km (about 62 mi) long but less than 1 m (about 3 ft) high. These waves pass under ships without being noticed. But when a tsunami reaches a shore, friction with the ocean bottom slows the wave. This causes the wave to grow to as much as 25 m (about 82 ft), destroying everything in its path.

During hurricanes and tropical storms, large domes of water called *storm surges*

Hurricane winds produce huge waves that East Coast surfers enjoy before the storm arrives.

form. Low air pressure at the storm's center causes ocean water to rise. Strong winds form huge waves on top of the storm surge, and they push this high water ahead of the storm. If the storm is moving toward land, it may send a wall of water up to 10 m (about 33 ft) high crashing onto the beach.

Another kind of wave is called a rogue (ROHG) wave. This is a huge wave, much higher than the waves around it. Many rogue waves form when large storm waves join together.

✔ **Name three different kinds of waves, and tell what causes them.**

Tsunamis, such as the one that hit Hilo, Hawai'i, in 1946, cause great damage to buildings along the shore. ▼

Even large boats can be sunk by rogue waves. ▼

Currents

Although waves are the most easily seen kind of ocean movement, currents move much more water. An ocean **current** is a stream of water that flows like a river through the ocean. Unlike waves, currents actually move water forward, sometimes for long distances.

Large ocean currents, known as *surface currents,* flow across the surface of the oceans. Surface currents are usually caused by prevailing winds. As a prevailing wind blows across the surface of the ocean, the water begins to move as a stream. Some surface currents can be hundreds of kilometers wide and hundreds of meters deep. A single one of these "ocean rivers" can move more water than the Amazon, the largest river in the world.

A surface current can carry cold water to warm regions. It can also carry warm water to cold regions. One surface current is the Gulf Stream. This warm current flows northeast from the Caribbean Sea, past the East Coast of the United States, and across the North Atlantic. Even after its long trip across the cold Atlantic, there is enough warm water in this current to warm the climate of Great Britain and northern Europe. That's why palm trees can grow along the southern coast of England.

The warm waters that form the Gulf Stream are shown in orange and red in this satellite photograph. Colder waters are shown in green and blue. ▼

▲ Rip currents (red arrows) may flow away from a beach at 8 km/h (about 5 mi/h). If you get caught in a rip current, swim parallel to the shore until you move out of the current. The water on both sides of the rip current flows toward the beach.

Surface currents aren't the only currents flowing through the oceans. *Shoreline currents* are local currents that run along the coast. Local winds and shifting beach materials may cause shoreline currents to change from day to day.

A *rip current* is a shoreline current that flows away from the beach. A rip current is often caused by a sand spit, a long ridge of sand that forms offshore near a beach. Ocean waves flow over the sand spit and toward the beach. But water from the waves can't flow back over the sand spit. The water piles up, trapped by the sand spit, until a small break opens up in the sand spit. The water then flows rapidly out through the opening, producing a strong current.

When waves strike a shore at an angle, they move water forward along the shore. This movement of water parallel to the beach produces another type of shoreline current, called a longshore current. Longshore currents carry large amounts of beach materials from one place to another.

Surface Currents

ARCTIC OCEAN

Greenland Current

ARCTIC OCEAN

North Pacific Drift

NORTH AMERICA

California Current

Labrador Current

North Atlantic Drift

Gulf Stream

ATLANTIC OCEAN

Canary Current

EURASIA

Oyashio Current

PACIFIC OCEAN

Kuroshio Current

AFRICA

North Equatorial Current

North Equatorial Current

Equatorial Countercurrent

South Equatorial Current

South Equatorial Current

Peru Current

SOUTH AMERICA

Brazil Current

ATLANTIC OCEAN

Benguela Current

Equatorial Countercurrent

South Equatorial Current

INDIAN OCEAN

AUSTRALIA

Equatorial Countercurrent

South Equatorial Current

East Australian Current

PACIFIC OCEAN

West Australian Current

West Wind Drift

West Wind Drift

ANTARCTICA

Warm current
Cold current

▲ This diagram shows how surface currents move. The red arrows show warm water, and the blue arrows show cold water.

Although wind blowing across the surface of an ocean can produce currents, these currents don't continue moving in the same direction as the wind. Earth's rotation causes ocean currents to bend to the right in the Northern Hemisphere and to the left in the Southern Hemisphere. The currents start moving in giant circles.

Not all ocean currents are caused by wind. Deep-ocean currents are caused by differences in water temperature. Cold water is heavier than warm water, so it sinks. The cold water then flows along the bottom of the ocean.

✔ **What causes ocean currents?**

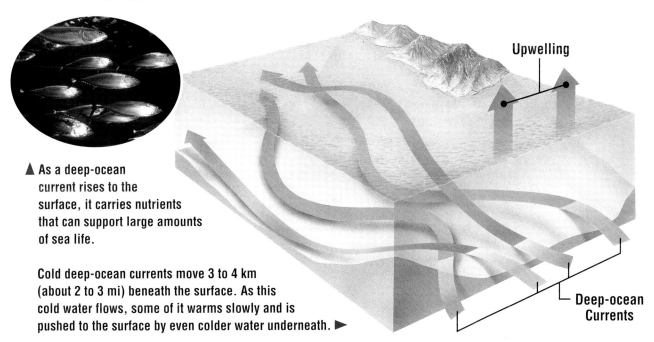

▲ As a deep-ocean current rises to the surface, it carries nutrients that can support large amounts of sea life.

Cold deep-ocean currents move 3 to 4 km (about 2 to 3 mi) beneath the surface. As this cold water flows, some of it warms slowly and is pushed to the surface by even colder water underneath. ▶

Upwelling

Deep-ocean Currents

Tides

Once or twice each day, ocean water rises and falls at every beach around the world. This repeated rise and fall in the level of the ocean is called the **tide**. Tides are caused by the pull of gravity of the sun and the moon on Earth's waters. Since the moon is closer to Earth than the sun, it has a greater effect on tides than the sun does.

The pull of the moon combines with Earth's rotation to produce traveling bulges of water. The moon's pull on the oceans is strongest on the side of Earth facing the moon. This causes Earth's shape to become slightly oval. Solid parts of Earth change very little. But the oceans bulge out on the side of Earth nearest the moon and on the side farthest from the moon. As Earth rotates, it pulls these bulges along.

The bulges of water on either side of Earth are called *high tides*. Low-water levels

▲ Very high tides occur every 14 days when the moon and sun line up. Weaker tides occur when the moon, the sun, and the Earth form a right angle.

between high tides are called *low tides*. Most coastal areas have one or two low tides and one or two high tides every 24 hours. Low and high tides occur at regular times, which can be predicted. The table shows high and

In the Bay of Fundy, between Maine and Nova Scotia, the difference between high and low tides can be as much as 20 m (about 66 ft)!

Tides for the Bay of Fundy

Date	Time	Ht.	Time	Ht.	Time	Ht.	Time	Ht.
1/15/2002	0354	5.4	1003	24.7	1623	3.8	2232	23.6
1/16/2002	0437	4.8	1045	25.2	1705	3.3	2313	24.1
1/17/2002	0519	4.4	1126	25.6	1746	2.8	2354	24.5
1/18/2002	0600	4.0	1206	25.9	1826	2.4		
1/19/2002	0034	24.8	0642	3.7	1247	26.0	1908	2.2
1/20/2002	0115	25.0	0725	3.5	1329	26.0	1950	2.2
1/21/2002	0158	25.1	0810	3.5	1414	25.7	2035	2.4

low tides during one week in Canada's Bay of Fundy. The Bay of Fundy is famous for its extremely high and low tides, so knowing when tides will occur is very important for boaters.

✔ **What causes tides?**

Summary

The ocean is in constant motion. Ocean waters move as waves, currents, and tides. Most waves are caused by wind. Currents are streams of water caused by winds or differences in water temperature. Tides are caused by the gravitational pull of the moon and sun on Earth's oceans.

Review

1. How does the water in an ocean wave move?

2. Compare the causes of surface currents with those of deep-ocean currents.

3. How do the moon's gravity and Earth's rotation affect tides?

4. **Critical Thinking** For a science fair project, a student dissolves food coloring in a cup of cold water. Then the student pours the cold, colored water into a glass of warm water. **Predict** what will happen to the colored water. Explain your prediction.

5. **Test Prep** Tides are caused by —
   A ocean currents
   B waves and the prevailing winds
   C the gravitational pull of the moon and sun on the oceans
   D hurricanes and other tropical storms

LINKS

MATH LINK

Describe Patterns Look at the tide table on page C106. Find the tides for January 20. At what times will high tide occur on that day? About how many hours apart are the two high tides?

WRITING LINK

Narrative Writing—Story Do some research about an ocean current. Where does the current begin? Where does it go? What does the current carry? How does the current affect the lands it touches? Then write a short story for your teacher about the current.

LANGUAGE ARTS LINK

Editing After you finish the first draft of your story about an ocean current, trade stories with a classmate for comments and corrections. Mark any errors in spelling or grammar. Then look for parts of the story that you like. Look also for parts that could be more exciting or that need to be explained better. Write any comments on the manuscript and give it back to your classmate.

TECHNOLOGY LINK

Learn more about the effects of waves and currents by visiting this Smithsonian Institution Internet site. **www.si.edu/harcourt/science**

 Smithsonian Institution®

How Do Oceans Interact with the Land?

In this lesson, you can . . .

INVESTIGATE the effect of waves on a beach.

LEARN ABOUT how the oceans affect the shoreline.

LINK to math, writing, technology, and other areas.

INVESTIGATE

The Effect of Waves on a Beach

Activity Purpose Every day ocean waves keep pounding against the shore. How do waves change a shore? In this activity you will **make a model** so you can **observe** the effect of waves on a beach.

Materials
- stream table
- sand
- water

Activity Procedure

1. Use sand to **make a model** of a beach at one end of the stream table. The beach should have a gentle slope. (Picture A)

2. Slowly add water to the stream table until it is about half full. Try not to disturb the beach.

◄ Ocean waves will soon destroy this sand castle.

Picture A

Picture B

3 Make a wave by lifting the sand end of the stream table about 2 cm above the tabletop and then dropping it. What do you **observe** about the beach and the water? Repeat this several times. **Record** your observations.

4 Repeat Steps 1–3, but this time build a beach that is much steeper than the first one. **Record** your observations. (Picture B)

Draw Conclusions

1. Use your observations to explain how waves affect a beach.

2. Does the slope of the beach matter? Explain.

3. **Scientists at Work** Scientists often **make a model** to study how natural processes work. How did your model help you **observe** how waves affect a beach? What couldn't you observe about wave action with your model?

Investigate Further If possible, study the shore of a pond, a lake, or an ocean in your area. What do you **observe** about the shore? **Hypothesize** how waves affect the shore. **Plan and conduct a simple experiment** to test your hypothesis.

Process Skill Tip

Not everyone can **observe** firsthand the effect of waves. But you can **make a model** to help you understand just how waves affect a beach.

How Ocean Waters Shape the Shore

FIND OUT

- how ocean waves and currents shape the shore
- how human activities can change the shore

VOCABULARY

shore
headland
tide pool
jetty

At the Shore

The area from where waves begin to break to the highest place they reach on the beach is called the shore. The **shore** is the area where the ocean and land meet and interact. Anyone who has lived near the ocean knows that the shore is a place of constant change.

As you saw in the investigation, waves change the shore in several ways. One is by grinding pebbles and rocks against the shore. This action erodes the bottoms of cliffs, causing them to break apart and fall into the ocean. Another way waves change the shore is through water pressure. Each breaking wave hurls tons of water at the shore. This water pressure loosens pebbles and small rocks, which the outgoing waves carry into the ocean.

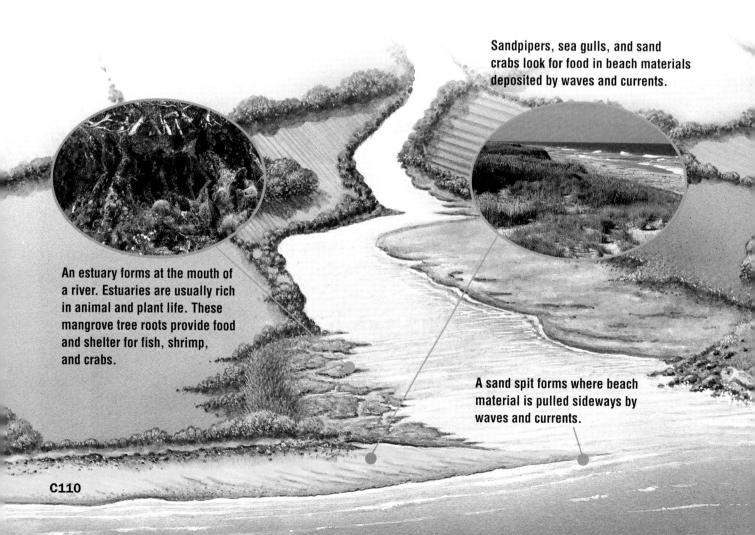

Sandpipers, sea gulls, and sand crabs look for food in beach materials deposited by waves and currents.

An estuary forms at the mouth of a river. Estuaries are usually rich in animal and plant life. These mangrove tree roots provide food and shelter for fish, shrimp, and crabs.

A sand spit forms where beach material is pulled sideways by waves and currents.

Where a shore is made of both soft rock and hard rock, erosion is uneven. Soft rock erodes faster than hard rock. Wave action may destroy the soft rock, forming small bays like those shown below. As the soft rock is washed away, the hard rock may be left as a rocky point, or **headland**. Sometimes the ocean cuts sea caves into a headland. If waves continue to erode the sea caves, a sea arch may form.

Currents also change a shore. If you've ever been swimming in the ocean, you may have noticed that when you came out of the water, you had to walk up and along the beach to the place where you left your towel. A longshore current carried you down the beach.

Longshore currents also move sand, pebbles, and shells along the shore. In places where the shore changes shape, a longshore current slows down and deposits beach materials. A new beach is formed, or the existing beach receives new sand and pebbles.

✔ **How do waves and currents change the shore?**

A **tide pool** is a pool of seawater found along a rocky shoreline. At high tide the pool is under water. This tide pool in California provides a habitat for a great variety of plants and animals.

Two sea caves have further eroded to form a sea arch like this one on Anacapa Island, in Channel Islands National Park, California.

Human Activities Affect the Shore

Human activities also change the shore. People in coastal communities often build structures to protect their beaches from erosion. These structures can block longshore currents and change the natural processes that erode and build up a shore.

At Cape Hatteras, along the coast of North Carolina, the Atlantic Ocean has eroded the beach so much that the lighthouse there was in danger of falling into the sea. The Cape Hatteras Lighthouse is one of the most famous lighthouses in the United States. To save the lighthouse, three small jetties, or groins were built along the water's edge to catch sand and build up the beach. A **jetty** is a wall-like structure made of rocks that sticks out into the ocean. Jetties are usually built on either side of an opening to a harbor. Groins are small jetties built along a beach.

A jetty protects a harbor by trapping sand and pebbles that normally flow down the coast with the longshore current. But jetties

These jetties were built to protect this beach from erosion. ▼

The Cape Hatteras Lighthouse was built in 1870 after many ships had sunk in the so-called Graveyard of the Atlantic. ▼

This was the Cape Hatteras Lighthouse in 1998. On parts of Hatteras Island, ocean waves wash away 4.3 m (about 15 ft) of beach each year. ▶

can also harm beaches. Although the beach above the jetty receives extra sand, beaches down the shore may lose their supply of sand and actually erode.

Cape Hatteras Lighthouse is safe for now. The lighthouse was moved farther from the ocean in 1999.

✔ **How do human activities affect the shore?**

Summary

The shore is changed by waves, currents, and human activities. Waves erode beaches and cliffs. Longshore currents deposit beach materials such as sand, pebbles, and shells along the shore. Jetties and other structures can affect the natural processes of shore change.

Review

1. How do waves erode beaches and cliffs?
2. How does a longshore current affect the shore?
3. What are two ways in which a jetty can affect a shore?
4. **Critical Thinking** A pier is built sticking out into the ocean. After a few years, sand builds up along one side of the pier. Explain why.
5. **Test Prep** An estuary is an area rich in plant and animal life that forms —
    A along a sandbar
    B along a jetty
    C at a headland
    D at the mouth of a river

Cumberland Island, Georgia, is a wide, beautiful barrier island. A barrier island is a long ridge of sand in the ocean running parallel to the shore. A barrier island gets its name from the fact that it blocks ocean waves and storm surges, protecting the low coastal mainland.

LINKS

MATH LINK

Estimate The Atlantic Ocean is eroding parts of Hatteras Island at the rate of 4.3 m per year. Estimate how many years it will take for 30 m of the island to be eroded.

WRITING LINK

Persuasive Writing—Opinion Take a stand for or against building jetties to save a beach. Prepare notes for a short speech explaining your point of view. Be sure to include facts and drawings or photographs to support your position. Present your speech to your classmates.

ART LINK

Shore Diagram Draw a picture showing how the ocean both erodes and builds up beaches.

SOCIAL STUDIES LINK

Shore Map Find a shore in your state to map. If you don't live near an ocean, map a large lake. Show natural features such as bays, estuaries, and beaches.

GO ONLINE TECHNOLOGY LINK

Learn more about the interactions of the ocean and the shore by visiting this Smithsonian Institution Internet site. **www.si.edu/harcourt/science**

Smithsonian Institution®

LESSON 4

How Do People Explore the Oceans and Use Ocean Resources?

In this lesson, you can . . .

INVESTIGATE how scientists measure ocean depths.

LEARN ABOUT how people explore the oceans and use ocean resources.

LINK to math, writing, literature, and technology.

This copper diving helmet was first used in about 1819. ▶

C114

How Scientists Measure Ocean Depths

Activity Purpose   In 1521 Portuguese explorer Ferdinand Magellan tried to measure the depth of the Pacific Ocean. He dropped 730 m (about 2400 ft) of weighted rope over the side of his ship. But this wasn't nearly enough rope to reach the bottom of the ocean. Today's scientists use *sonar*, or sound wave devices, to determine how deep the ocean is. In this activity you will learn about two ways to **measure** the depth of water—Magellan's way and a more modern way.

Materials

- shoe box
- sand, pebbles, small rocks
- construction paper
- scissors
- ruler
- string
- weight
- calculator

Activity Procedure

1   **Make a model** of the ocean floor by pouring sand and pebbles into the shoe box. Then scatter a few small rocks on top of the sand. (Picture A)

2   Cut a piece of construction paper large enough to cover the top of the box. This will stand for the sea surface.

3   With a pencil and ruler, draw a grid on the paper 4 squares wide by 8 squares long. Number the squares 1 through 32, and tape the lid onto the box. Tie the weight to a piece of string about twice as long as the box is deep.

4 Make a hole in the first square in any row and lower the weighted end of the string until the weight just touches the ocean floor. (Picture A)

5 Hold the string at sea level. **Measure** the length of string you pinched off to find the depth of the ocean. **Record** your measurement. Repeat Steps 4 and 5 for the remaining squares in that row.

6 Now copy the Sonar Data table. The "Time" is the number of seconds it takes for a sound to travel from a boat to the bottom of the ocean and back to the boat.

7 Use a calculator to multiply the Location 1 time by 1500 m/s (the speed of sound in water). Then divide the product by 2. This number is the depth of the water in meters at Location 1. This one has been done for you.

8 Repeat Step 7 for each location in the table. Then make a line graph of the depths. The graph will be a profile of the ocean floor.

Picture A

Sonar Data		
Location	Time (s)	Depth (m)
1	1.8	1350
2	2.0	
3	3.6	
4	4.5	
5	5.3	
6	2.3	
7	3.1	
8	4.6	
9	5.0	
10	5.2	

Draw Conclusions

1. Why do you think scientists today use sonar rather than weighted ropes to **measure** the depth of the ocean?

2. When using sonar, why must you divide each product by 2 to calculate the depth of the water?

3. **Scientists at Work** How could a scientist use sonar to **measure** the size of large objects on the ocean floor?

Investigate Further How could you find the depth of a pond, lake, or river? **Plan and conduct a simple investigation** to find out.

> **Process Skill Tip**
>
> You **measure** when you use a tool to find how deep the water is.

Exploring the Oceans and Using Ocean Resources

Exploring the Ocean

FIND OUT

- about ocean exploration
- about *Alvin*, the submersible that helped find RMS *Titanic*
- how people use ocean resources

VOCABULARY

scuba

submersible

sonar

desalination

Did you know that more than 70 percent of Earth is covered with water? Viewed from space, the continents we live on seem like big islands with oceans around them. People have been exploring the oceans for thousands of years. Early peoples took trips in small boats to search for food, to move to new homes, and to find better trade routes. Some went just for adventure. The time line below shows some of the ways in which people have explored the oceans in the past 600 years.

Scientists and explorers have been studying the oceans for hundreds of years. People designed diving suits as early as the

The voyage of HMS *Challenger* in 1872 started the modern science of oceanography (oh•shuhn•AWG•ruh•fee) —the scientific study of the oceans.

1400s	1500s	1600s	1700s	1800s

This diving suit was designed in the 1400s.

Sir Edmond Halley, an English astronomer, built this diving bell in 1690. Air was sent down to the bell using barrels and leather tubes. The bell shape trapped air for the divers to use.

1400s, and by 1690, divers could use Sir Edmond Halley's diving bell to explore to a depth of 18 m (about 60 ft) below sea level.

Detailed studies of the oceans began in 1872 with the voyage of the British ship HMS *Challenger*. Led by C. Wyville Thomson, six scientists spent about four years at sea. They took thousands of samples and measurements of the oceans. They studied the chemistry of sea water and collected ocean plants, animals, and minerals.

With simple methods like you used in the investigation, Thomson and his staff achieved many firsts. Using a weighted line and a steam engine, they measured a water depth of 8185 m (about 26,850 ft) in the western Pacific. They also captured and classified 4717 new species of marine life. The scientific reports of their expedition filled 50 books.

Today's scientists use many different technologies to explore the oceans. They dive beneath the water wearing **scuba** equipment. (The letters *s-c-u-b-a* stand for *self-contained **u**nderwater **b**reathing **a**pparatus*.) They travel in small, underwater vehicles called **submersibles**. Satellites are used to study ocean currents from space, and **sonar** (a device that uses sound waves) is used to map the ocean floor.

✔ **What technologies do scientists use to explore the oceans?**

In 1960 Jacques Piccard and Donald Walsh went down in the *Trieste II* to the deepest place in the Pacific Ocean. They reached a depth of about 10,910 m (35,800 ft). At this depth the top of Mount Everest would still be about 1525 m (5000 ft) below the ocean's surface.

Today, satellites can measure an ocean's salt content, temperature, wave heights, and current flows from thousands of kilometers in space. Sensors can even show where tiny organisms called plankton are found in ocean waters.

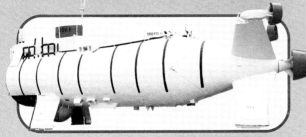

1900–1935	1935–1960	1960–2000

The Aqua-lung, an early form of scuba, was invented in 1942 by French explorer Jacques Cousteau. With scuba gear, a diver can move freely about underwater to a depth of about 60 m (200 ft).

The submersible *Alvin* has played an important role in exploring ocean depths. To reach the *Titanic* in 1986, it had to travel nearly 4000 m (about 13,000 ft) beneath the ocean's surface.

Submersibles

One of the best-known submersibles is *Alvin*, named in honor of ocean scientist Allyn Vine. In 1956 Vine convinced the United States government that scientists needed deep-diving vessels that could hold small crews. By the 1960s *Alvin* was exploring the oceans.

In 1977 scientists in *Alvin* discovered underwater vents along the Mid-Atlantic Ridge. In 1986 *Alvin* was used to explore the wreckage of the sunken ship RMS *Titanic*.

Alvin may have been the first submersible to explore *Titanic*, but it wasn't the last.

During the 1990s a team of French and American explorers used a newer submersible, *Nautile*, to continue the job *Alvin* started.

Nautile first visited the *Titanic* wreck in 1987, bringing up some objects from the site. In the 1990s even more objects were brought up, including a large part of the sunken ship itself.

THE INSIDE STORY

Alvin

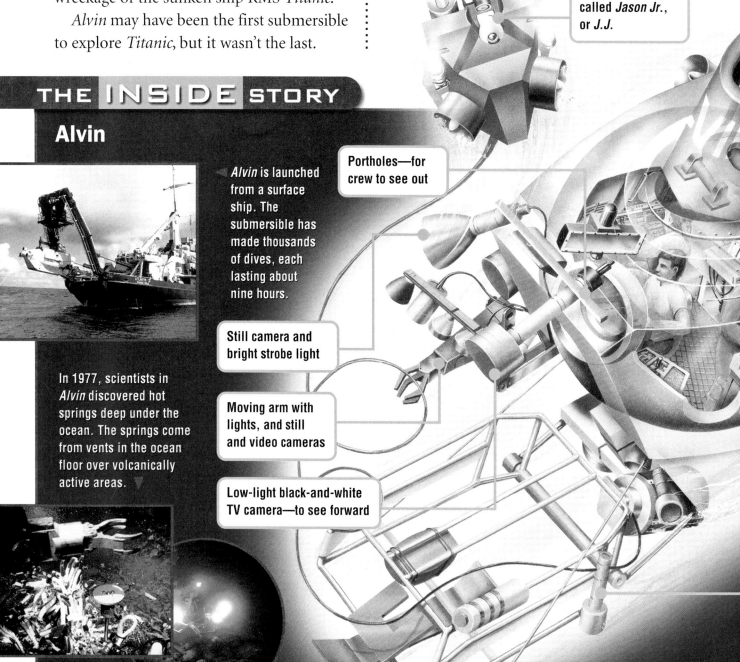

Remote-controlled underwater robot called *Jason Jr.*, or *J.J.*

Alvin is launched from a surface ship. The submersible has made thousands of dives, each lasting about nine hours.

Portholes—for crew to see out

Still camera and bright strobe light

Moving arm with lights, and still and video cameras

Low-light black-and-white TV camera—to see forward

In 1977, scientists in *Alvin* discovered hot springs deep under the ocean. The springs come from vents in the ocean floor over volcanically active areas.

With space for crews of three—one pilot and two scientists each—*Alvin* and *Nautile* can work inside sea caves, shipwrecks, and other small spaces.

Crewed submersibles allow scientists to observe underwater objects up close. They have been able to make important scientific discoveries, as well as explore sunken ships.

But in the future, underwater exploration may be done with small, crewless submersibles. These underwater robots can fit into places too small for *Alvin* or *Nautile*. And they can dive deeper and stay longer on the ocean floor.

✔ **What kinds of places have scientists used submersibles to explore?**

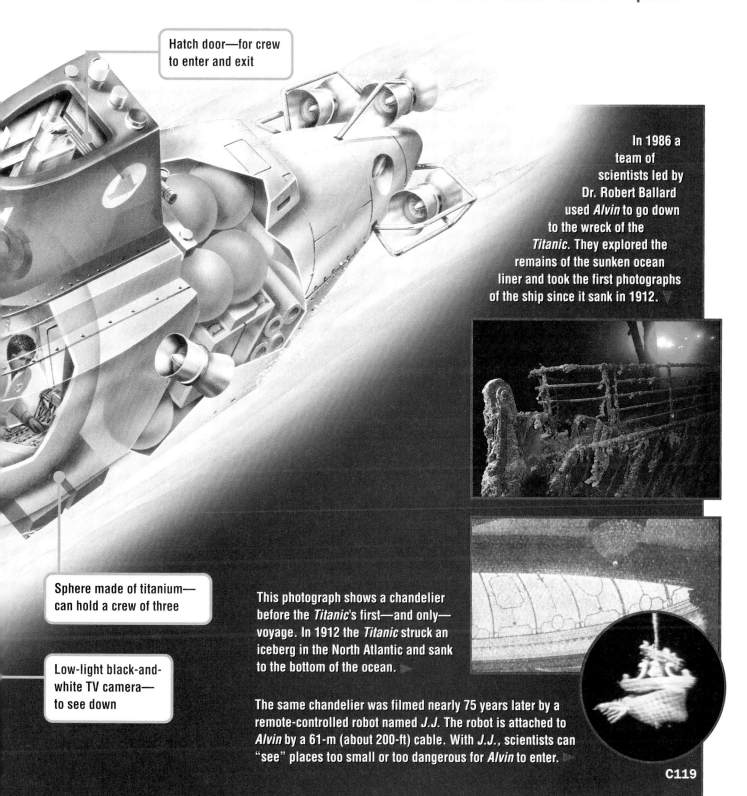

Hatch door—for crew to enter and exit

Sphere made of titanium—can hold a crew of three

Low-light black-and-white TV camera—to see down

In 1986 a team of scientists led by Dr. Robert Ballard used *Alvin* to go down to the wreck of the *Titanic*. They explored the remains of the sunken ocean liner and took the first photographs of the ship since it sank in 1912. ▼

This photograph shows a chandelier before the *Titanic*'s first—and only—voyage. In 1912 the *Titanic* struck an iceberg in the North Atlantic and sank to the bottom of the ocean. ▷

The same chandelier was filmed nearly 75 years later by a remote-controlled robot named *J.J.* The robot is attached to *Alvin* by a 61-m (about 200-ft) cable. With *J.J.*, scientists can "see" places too small or too dangerous for *Alvin* to enter. ▷

Using Ocean Resources

The importance of the oceans is not just in the discoveries they hold for scientists. The oceans contain huge amounts of natural resources. Ocean waters are filled with plants and animals. The ocean floor contains many minerals. Gas and oil are buried deep beneath the ocean floor. And in some places, sea water itself has become an important resource.

Among the ocean's most important resources are its fish and shellfish. Millions of people around the world feed their families by fishing from small boats. Others fish for large companies on factory ships—huge boats where fish can be cleaned, processed, and canned or frozen right on board.

Sea plants are another ocean resource. People eat some kinds of seaweed as food. Carrageenin (kar•uh•JEE•nuhn), a product made from seaweed, is used in foods, toothpaste, hand creams, and fertilizer.

As resources on land become scarce, people are beginning to mine underwater mineral deposits. Sand, gravel, and shells are easily obtained near the shore. Hundreds of millions of tons are dredged from the sea each year and used for road construction and building materials. Minerals containing iron, copper, manganese, nickel, and cobalt can be taken from lumps, or nodules, lying on the sea floor. These deep-sea nodules are difficult to mine, however, since they are located at depths of 4000 m (about 13,125 ft) or more.

Petroleum and natural gas are pumped from beneath the ocean floor using huge offshore drilling rigs. Almost a quarter of the world's petroleum and natural gas now comes from under the ocean.

Another useful resource, salt, is dissolved in the sea water itself. Since ancient times people have used the process of evaporation to remove salt from sea water. Much of the world's salt is still obtained using this natural process.

There is still another valuable ocean resource—water. In some parts of the world, freshwater supplies are so limited that water is taken from the ocean. The salt is removed from sea water by **desalination**. In one method, sea water is evaporated, leaving the minerals behind. The water vapor is then cooled and condensed back into fresh water. In another desalination method, sea water is passed through a plastic film that allows pure water, but not the dissolved salts, to go through.

✔ **What resources do people take from the ocean?**

Offshore drilling rigs like this one may stand in water as deep as 300 m (about 1000 ft). ▶

▲ Desalination plants like this one provide water for drinking or industry. Right now the cost is usually too high to use desalinated water for farm irrigation.

Summary

Ocean exploration has a long history. Today's ocean scientists have a wide range of technology that they can use, including scuba equipment, submersibles, satellites, and sonar. The oceans also contain valuable natural resources such as fish, petroleum, minerals, and sea water itself.

Review

1. What did the crew of the *Challenger* study?
2. Why are submersibles such as *Alvin* valuable to ocean scientists?
3. What mineral resources are found in or beneath the ocean?
4. **Critical Thinking** The deeper you go in the ocean, the greater the water pressure. Use logical reasoning to **infer** why.
5. **Test Prep** Which word does NOT belong with the others?
   A seaweed
   B salt
   C manganese
   D iron

LINKS

MATH LINK

Solve Problems A typical dive with *Alvin* lasts about 9 hours. Of these 9 hours, 30 minutes are spent launching the craft. Another 30 minutes are spent recovering it from the water. The descent to the ocean floor takes $2\frac{1}{2}$ hours, and the ascent back to the surface takes another $2\frac{1}{2}$ hours. How long do the scientists have for research?

WRITING LINK

Narrative Writing—Story Choose an ocean resource to research. Find out more about this resource, including how it is obtained and how it is used. Then write a science fiction story for your class that describes a world where that resource has become scarce.

LITERATURE LINK

***Exploring the* Titanic** The complete story of the *Titanic* expedition is told in this book by Robert D. Ballard. In 1985 Ballard and his team discovered the remains of the *Titanic* on the ocean floor. A year later the team returned to explore the ship in the submersible *Alvin*.

TECHNOLOGY LINK

Learn more about ocean exploration by viewing *Jacques Cousteau* on the **Harcourt Science Newsroom Video.**

Saltwater Agriculture

Who would grow crops in a desert? Scientists would, and they are using salt water to do it.

By the Sea

The first major use of salt water for growing crops was in Israel. At the end of World War II, Hugo and Elisabeth Boyko decided to live there. Elisabeth was a horticulturist, an expert in growing certain plants, and Hugo was an ecologist.

The Boykos used their skills to landscape a town near the Red Sea. They wanted to make it prettier so that more people would move there. Growing plants in the seaside town was a challenge. Most plants need rich soil and fresh water to grow, but here the land was sandy and the only water was from the sea. They pumped salt water from the sea to irrigate, or water, their plants. Many plants are killed by salt water, but the Boykos noticed that some plants survived in spite of the salt.

Since then other scientists have continued the Boykos' work. Some have teamed up with desert farmers in Mexico, India, and other countries to build experimental farms that practice saltwater agriculture.

A Growing Challenge

Why grow crops in a desert? And why use salty seawater instead of fresh water from

Glasswort is a halophyte. It can grow in salty soil.

C122

This photograph shows a landscaped town along the Red Sea.

rivers or lakes? There are some very important reasons.

The world's population is increasing, so there are more and more people to feed. But Earth's supplies of good farmland and fresh water are shrinking. Every year it gets harder to raise enough food for everyone. Where could farmers find additional land and water? Areas of desert near an ocean seem like an excellent choice.

Saltwater Crops

Corn, wheat, rice, potatoes, and soybeans are the main crops that people eat. Salt water kills them all. What else is there? Halophytes. Halophytes are plants that grow in the wild and survive in salty soil. In fact, halophytes absorb salt and store it inside themselves. That's why some of them taste so salty.

One halophyte that could be used for food is called glasswort. This leafless plant can be fed to livestock. Its seeds contain protein and oil, and the oil has a nutlike taste. However, glasswort isn't the perfect crop—yet. Glasswort is so salty that it makes livestock thirsty. They have to drink more water than usual, which is not a good way to save fresh water, especially in a desert. Can scientists develop a less salty glasswort? Agronomists are trying.

THINK ABOUT IT

1. Why would it be useful to farm deserts near oceans?
2. What advantages and disadvantages are there to growing halophytes?

CAREERS
HYDROLOGIST

What They Do
Hydrologists test drinking water, issue flood warnings, check underground water supplies, and protect water in other ways. Many work in government agencies, city or state offices, consulting firms, and waste-treatment plants.

Education and Training
A person wishing to become a hydrologist needs to study physical or natural science or engineering and take courses in soils, marine biology, or other scientific fields. Math and computer skills are also helpful.

WEB LINK
For Science and Technology updates, visit the Harcourt Internet site.
www.harcourtschool.com

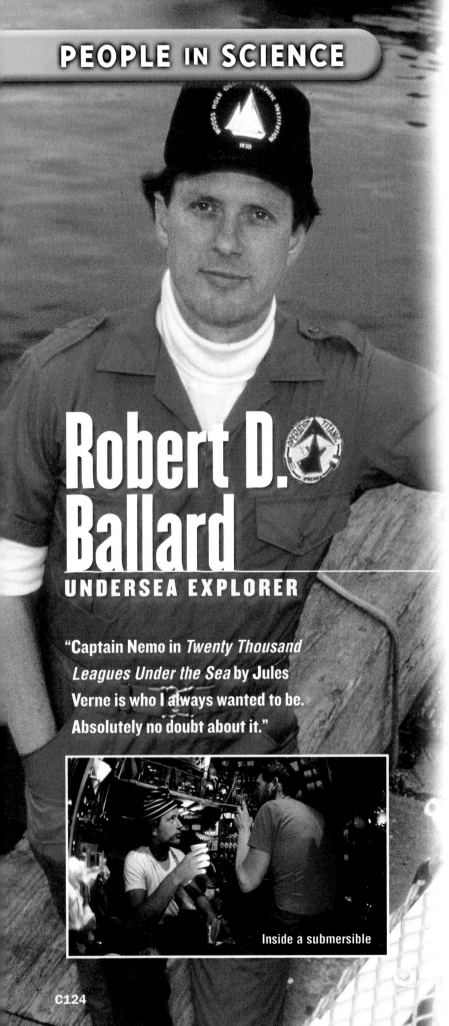

Robert D. Ballard

UNDERSEA EXPLORER

"Captain Nemo in *Twenty Thousand Leagues Under the Sea* by Jules Verne is who I always wanted to be. Absolutely no doubt about it."

Inside a submersible

Undersea explorer Robert D. Ballard made headlines around the world when he and his crew located the wreck of the R.M.S. *Titanic*. Although most people know of Dr. Ballard for making this discovery, his fellow scientists know him for discovering deep-ocean life forms and geologic processes never seen before.

Although geologists had hypothesized that thermal vents existed, no one had predicted that there would be so many kinds of organisms there. Dr. Ballard observed huge blood-red worms without eyes or mouths, clusters of giant clams, blind crabs, and other strange animals. These animals depend on bacteria, not on plants, for food.

Dr. Ballard's team is also recognized for discovering that all the water of the oceans is recycled over time through Earth's crust. This discovery has helped scientists explain why sea water is full of minerals.

Interested in becoming an undersea explorer from the time he was a boy, Dr. Ballard is thankful to the many people who taught and encouraged him throughout his career. "You need to pick out certain people you have great respect for and listen to them," he says. "At every critical point in my life, when I was ready to quit, I can point to someone who said, 'Keep it up.'"

THINK ABOUT IT

1. Why was discovering that all the water of the oceans is recycled through Earth's crust important?

2. Why is working as part of a team important to scientists?

WATER WORLD

What happens when waters meet?

Materials

- water
- 200-mL beaker
- food coloring
- hot plate
- tongs
- water-filled aquarium

Procedure

❶ Fill the beaker half-full of water. Add food coloring to the water.

❷ Using the hot plate, gently warm the water in the beaker.

❸ Your teacher or another adult will use the tongs to lower the beaker straight down into the aquarium filled with cold water.

❹ Observe the hot, colored water as it leaves the beaker.

Draw Conclusions

Describe what you observed. From your observations, what conclusions can you draw about areas in the ocean where warm currents flow through cooler waters?

OIL AND WATER

Why did ancient sailors use oil to calm the seas near their ships?

Materials

- glass bread pan
- water
- food coloring
- drinking straw
- cooking oil

Procedure

❶ Fill the glass pan about half-full of water.

❷ Add several drops of food coloring to the water.

❸ Using the straw, gently blow across the surface of the water.

❹ Now slowly pour oil into the water until it forms a layer of oil about 1 cm thick on top of the water.

❺ Using the straw, blow gently across the surface again.

Draw Conclusions

Compare the waves produced in Step 3 with those produced in Step 5. What do you conclude to be the cause of any differences in the waves? Why would sailors pour oil on the water during rough weather?

Vocabulary Review

Use the terms below to complete the sentences. The page numbers in ( ) tell you where to look in the chapter if you need help.

salinity (C97)   headland (C111)

water pressure (C97)   jetty (C112)

wave (C102)   scuba (C117)

current (C104)   submersible (C117)

tide (C106)   sonar (C117)

shore (C110)   desalination (C120)

tide pool (C111)

1. The ____, which is the repeated rise and fall in the level of the ocean, is caused by the pull of gravity of the moon and the sun.

2. The area where the ocean and the land meet and interact is the ____.

3. Scientists can use self-contained underwater breathing apparatus, or ____, equipment to dive beneath the water.

4. In an ocean ____, a stream of water moves through the ocean like a river, but in a ____, water moves up and down in a circular motion.

5. A ____ is a small underwater vehicle used to explore the ocean.

6. The weight of overlying water is called ____.

7. Scientists can use ____ to map the ocean floor.

8. A pool of sea water found along a rocky shore is called a ____.

9. A ____ is a rocky point that juts out into the ocean.

10. A ____ is a wall-like structure made of rocks that sticks out into the ocean.

11. The process of ____ removes the salt from sea water.

12. The saltiness of ocean water is its ____.

Connect Concepts

Use terms from the Word Bank to complete the concept map below.

wave   tide   submersible

scuba   shore

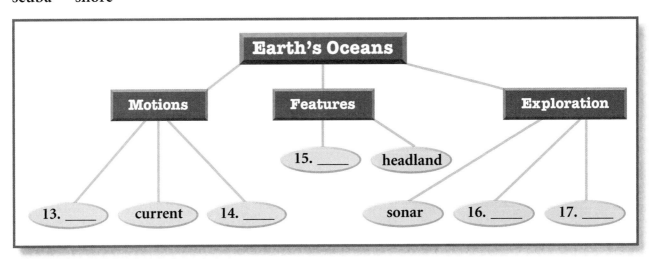

Check Understanding

Write the letter of the best choice.

18. A tsunami is a wave caused by —
  A an earthquake   **C** a storm surge
  B a high tide   **D** an ocean current

19. The main cause of tides is —
  F ocean waves
  G the moon's gravity
  H the sun's energy
  J longshore currents

20. Deep-ocean currents are caused by —
  A volcanoes deep under water
  B prevailing winds
  C the Earth's rotation
  D differences in water temperature

21. Shoreline currents are caused by —
  F local winds and conditions
  G prevailing winds
  H the saltiness of the water
  J sandspits

22. Most of the ocean floor is —
  A continental shelf
  B continental slope
  C abyssal plain
  D mid-ocean ridge

23. Detailed study of the oceans began with —
  F the discovery of the *Titanic*
  G the invention of scuba gear
  H the voyage of the *Challenger*
  J the scientists of the *Trieste*

24. Earth's oceans include the —
  A Atlantic   **C** Indian
  B Pacific   **D** all of the above

25. *Alvin* is a ____ that scientists used to discover hot springs deep under the ocean.
  F sailboat   **H** satellite
  G submersible   **J** robot

Critical Thinking

26. Suppose you drop a ball into the ocean in a place where there is no current. Will waves move the ball quickly away, or will it bob in place? Explain.

27. Suppose you have the choice of buying one of two houses. Both houses are built near the beach. One is 50 m from the ocean. The other is 100 m from the ocean. Which house would you choose? Explain.

28. Suppose you are an ocean miner. Tell how you might obtain a mineral that is on the ocean bottom, 1000 m below the surface.

Process Skills Review

29. How can you **make a model** of a tide pool?

30. Which method of **measuring** works better to determine the depth of the ocean—sonar or weighted ropes? Explain.

Performance Assessment

Waves

Using construction paper, glue, and two pieces of string, make a model to compare the way *energy* in waves travels with the way *water* in waves travels.

There are many places where you can find out more about processes that change the Earth. You can study weather and some of these Earth-changing forces at the places below. You'll also have fun while you learn.

National Weather Service Baltimore-Washington Forecast Office

WHAT A weather station where weather conditions are monitored and forecasts are made

WHERE Sterling, Virginia

WHAT CAN YOU DO THERE? Tour the weather station, see the equipment used to monitor the weather, and learn how weather forecasts are made.

Mammoth Cave National Park

WHAT The longest recorded cave system in the world, with more than 336 miles explored and mapped

WHERE Mammoth Cave, Kentucky

WHAT CAN YOU DO THERE? Take the tour of this cave system, see the many geologic formations, and learn how this cave was made.

(GO ONLINE) Plan Your Own Expeditions

If you can't visit the National Weather Service Baltimore-Washington Forecast Office or Mammoth Cave National Park, visit a weather station or a cave near you. Or log on to The Learning Site at **www.harcourtschool.com** to visit these science sites and other places to find out more about processes that change the Earth.

References

Science Handbook

Using Science Tools

Using a Hand Lens

A hand lens magnifies objects, or makes them look larger than they are.

1. Hold the hand lens about 12 centimeters (5 in.) from your eye.

2. Bring the object toward you until it comes into focus.

Using a Thermometer

A thermometer measures the temperature of air and most liquids.

1. Place the thermometer in the liquid. Don't touch the thermometer any more than you need to. Never stir the liquid with the thermometer. If you are measuring the temperature of the air, make sure that the thermometer is not in line with a direct light source.

2. Move so that your eyes are even with the liquid in the thermometer.

3. If you are measuring a material that is not being heated or cooled, wait about two minutes for the reading to become stable. Find the scale line that meets the top of the liquid in the thermometer, and read the temperature.

4. If the material you are measuring is being heated or cooled, you will not be able to wait before taking your measurements. Measure as quickly as you can.

Caring for and Using a Microscope

A microscope is another tool that magnifies objects. A microscope can increase the detail you see by increasing the number of times an object is magnified.

Caring for a Microscope

- Always use two hands when you carry a microscope.

- Never touch any of the lenses of a microscope with your fingers.

Using a Microscope

1. Raise the eyepiece as far as you can using the coarse-adjustment knob. Place your slide on the stage.

2. Always start by using the lowest power. The lowest-power lens is usually the shortest. Start with the lens in the lowest position it can go without touching the slide.

3. Look through the eyepiece, and begin adjusting it upward with the coarse-adjustment knob. When the slide is close to being in focus, use the fine-adjustment knob.

4. When you want to use a higher-power lens, first focus the slide under low power. Then, watching carefully to make sure that the lens will not hit the slide, turn the higher-power lens into place. Use only the fine-adjustment knob when looking through the higher-power lens.

You may use a Brock microscope. This is a sturdy microscope that has only one lens.

1. Place the object to be viewed on the stage.

2. Look through the eyepiece, and begin raising the tube until the object comes into focus.

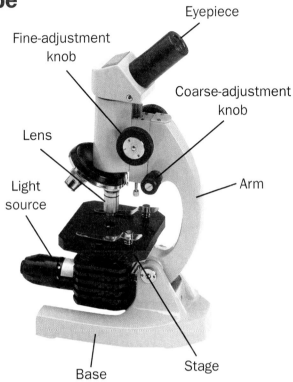

A Light Microscope

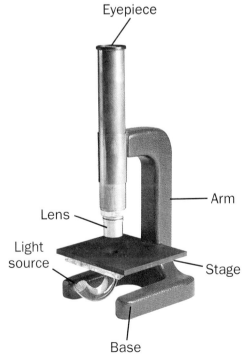

A Brock Microscope

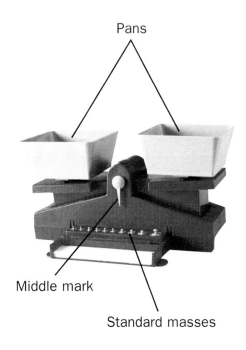

Pans

Middle mark

Standard masses

Using a Balance

Use a balance to measure an object's mass. Mass is the amount of matter an object has.

1. Look at the pointer on the base to make sure the empty pans are balanced.

2. Place the object you wish to measure in the left pan.

3. Add the standard masses to the other pan. As you add masses, you should see the pointer move. When the pointer is at the middle mark, the pans are balanced.

4. Add the numbers on the masses you used. The total is the mass in grams of the object you measured.

Using a Spring Scale

Use a spring scale to measure forces such as the pull of gravity on objects. You measure weight and other forces in units called newtons (N).

Measuring the Weight of an Object

1. Hook the spring scale to the object.

2. Lift the scale and object with a smooth motion. Do not jerk them upward.

3. Wait until any motion of the spring comes to a stop. Then read the number of newtons from the scale.

Measuring the Force to Move an Object

1. With the object resting on a table, hook the spring scale to it.

2. Pull the object smoothly across the table. Do not jerk the object.

3. As you pull, read the number of newtons you are using to pull the object.

Beaker   **Graduate**

Measuring Liquids

Use a beaker, a measuring cup, or a graduate to measure liquids accurately.

1. Pour the liquid you want to measure into a measuring container. Put your measuring container on a flat surface, with the measuring scale facing you.

2. Look at the liquid through the container. Move so that your eyes are even with the surface of the liquid in the container.

3. To read the volume of the liquid, find the scale line that is even with the surface of the liquid.

4. If the surface of the liquid is not exactly even with a line, estimate the volume of the liquid. Decide which line the liquid is closer to, and use that number.

Using a Ruler or Meterstick

Use a ruler or meterstick to measure distances and to find lengths of objects.

1. Place the zero mark or end of the ruler or meterstick next to one end of the distance or object you want to measure.

2. On the ruler or meterstick, find the place next to the other end of the distance or object.

3. Look at the scale on the ruler or meterstick. This will show the distance you want or the length of the object.

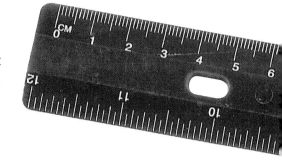

Using a Timing Device

Use a timing device such as a stopwatch to measure time.

1. Reset the stopwatch to zero.

2. When you are ready to begin timing, press start.

3. As soon as you are ready to stop timing, press stop.

4. The numbers on the dial or display show how many minutes, seconds, and parts of seconds have passed.

Glossary

As you read your science book, you will notice that new or unfamiliar words have been respelled to help you pronounce them quickly while you are reading. Those respellings are *phonetic respellings*. In this Glossary you will see a different kind of respelling. Here, diacritical marks are used, as they are used in dictionaries. *Diacritical respellings* provide a more precise pronunciation of the word.

When you see the ′ mark after a syllable, pronounce that syllable with more force than the other syllables. The page number at the end of the definition tells where to find the word in your book. The boldfaced letters in the examples in the Pronunciation Key that folows show how these letters are pronounced in the respellings after each glossary word.

PRONUNCIATION KEY

a	**a**dd, m**a**p	m	**m**ove, see**m**	u	**u**p, d**o**ne		
ā	**a**ce, r**a**te	n	**n**ice, ti**n**	û(r)	b**ur**n, t**er**m		
â(r)	**ca**re, **ai**r	ng	ri**ng**, so**ng**	yo͞o	**f**use, **f**ew		
ä	p**a**lm, f**a**ther	o	**o**dd, h**o**t	v	**v**ain, e**v**e		
b	**b**at, ru**b**	ō	**o**pen, s**o**	w	**w**in, a**w**ay		
ch	**ch**eck, cat**ch**	ô	**or**der, j**a**w	y	**y**et, **y**earn		
d	**d**og, ro**d**	oi	**oi**l, b**oy**	z	**z**est, mu**s**e		
e	**e**nd, p**e**t	ou	p**ou**t, n**ow**	zh	vi**s**ion, plea**s**ure		
ē	**e**qual, tr**ee**	o͝o	t**oo**k, f**u**ll	ə	the schwa, an		
f	**f**it, hal**f**	o͞o	p**oo**l, f**oo**d		unstressed vowel		
g	**g**o, lo**g**	p	**p**it, sto**p**		representing the sound		
h	**h**ope, **h**ate	r	**r**un, poo**r**		spelled		
i	**i**t, g**i**ve	s	**s**ee, pa**ss**		*a* in **a**bove		
ī	**i**ce, wr**i**te	sh	**s**ure, ru**sh**		*e* in sick**e**n		
j	**j**oy, le**dge**	t	**t**alk, si**t**		*i* in poss**i**ble		
k	**c**ool, ta**k**e	th	**th**in, bo**th**		*o* in mel**o**n		
l	**l**ook, ru**l**e	t͟h	**th**is, ba**th**e		*u* in circ**u**s		

Other symbols:
- • separates words into syllables
- ′ indicates heavier stress on a syllable
- ′ indicates light stress on a syllable

acceleration [ak•sel′ər•ā′shən] A change in motion caused by unbalanced forces or a change in velocity **(F13, F35)**

acid rain [as′id rān′] Precipitation resulting from pollution condensing into clouds and falling to Earth **(B99)**

action force [ak′shən fôrs′] The first force in the third law of motion **(F43)**

air mass [âr′ mas′] A large body of air that has nearly the same temperature and humidity throughout **(C75)**

air pressure [âr′ presh′ər] The weight of air **(C65)**

alveoli [al•vē′ə•lē] Tiny air sacs located at the ends of bronchi in the lungs **(A18)**

amphibians [am•fib′ē•ənz] Animals that have moist skin and no scales **(A44)**

angiosperm [an′jē•ō•spûrm′] A flowering plant **(A103)**

asexual reproduction [ā•sek′shoo•əl rē′prə•duk′shən] Reproduction by simple cell division **(A67)**

asteroids [as′tə•roidz] Chunks of rock that look like giant potatoes in space **(D16)**

atmosphere [at′məs•fir] The layer of air that surrounds Earth **(C64)**

atom [at′əm] The smallest unit of an element that has all the properties of that element **(E40)**

axis [ak′sis] An imaginary line that passes through Earth's center and its North and South Poles **(D7)**

balanced forces [bal′ənst fôrs′əz] The forces acting on an object that are equal in size and opposite in direction, canceling each other out **(F12)**

biomass [bī′ō•mas′] Organic matter, such as wood, that is living or was recently alive **(F110)**

biome [bī′ōm′] A large-scale ecosystem **(B64)**

birds [bûrdz] Vertebrates with feathers **(A45)**

bone marrow [bōn′ mar′ō] A connective tissue that produces red and white blood cells **(A24)**

capillaries [kap′ə•ler′ēz] The smallest blood vessels **(A17)**

carbon–oxygen cycle [kär′bən ok′sə•jən sī′kəl] The process by which carbon and oxygen cycle among plants, animals, and the environment **(B8)**

cell [sel] The basic unit of structure and function of all living things **(A6)**

cell membrane [sel′ mem′brān′] The thin covering that encloses a cell and holds its parts together **(A8)**

chemical bonds [kem′i•kəl bondz′] The forces that join atoms to each other **(F98)**

chlorophyll [klôr′ə•fil′] A pigment, or coloring matter, that helps plants use light energy to produce sugars **(A96)**

chromosome [krō′mə•sōm′] A threadlike strand of DNA inside the nucleus **(A65)**

classification [klas′ə•fə•kā′shən] The grouping of things by using a set of rules **(A38)**

climate [klī′mit] The average of all weather conditions through all seasons over a period of time **(C80)**

climate zone [klī′mit zōn′] A region throughout which yearly patterns of temperature, rainfall, and amount of sunlight are similar **(B64)**

climax community [klī′maks′ kə•myōō′nə•tē] The last stage of succession **(B93)**

combustibility [kəm•bus′tə•bil′ə•tē] The chemical property of being able to burn **(E24)**

comets [kom′its] Balls of ice and rock that circle the sun from two regions beyond the orbit of Pluto **(D16)**

community [kə•myōō′nə•tē] All the populations of organisms living together in an environment **(B28)**

competition [kom′pə•tish′ən] The contest among organisms for the limited resources of an ecosystem **(B42)**

compound [kom′pound] A substance made of the atoms of two or more different elements **(E48)**

condensation [kon′dən•sā′shən] The process by which a gas changes back into a liquid **(B14, C67, E17)**

conduction [kən•duk′shən] The direct transfer of heat between objects that touch **(F85)**

conductor [kən•duk′tər] A material that conducts electrons easily **(F70)**

conserving [kən•sûrv′ing] The saving or protecting of resources **(B104)**

consumer [kən•sōō′mər] An organism in a community that must eat to get the energy it needs **(B34)**

continental drift [kon′tə•nen′təl drift′] A theory of how Earth's continents move over its surface **(C22)**

convection [kən•vek′shən] The transfer of heat as a result of the mixing of a liquid or a gas **(F85)**

core [kôr] The center of the Earth **(C14)**

corona [kə•rō′nə] The sun's atmosphere **(D41)**

crust [krust] The thin, outer layer of Earth **(C14)**

current [kûr′ənt] A stream of water that flows like a river through the ocean **(C104)**

cytoplasm [sīt′ō•plaz′əm] A jellylike substance containing many chemicals that keep a cell functioning **(A9)**

decomposer [dē′kəm•pōz′ər] Consumer that breaks down the tissues of dead organisms **(B35)**

density [den′sə•tē] The concentration of matter in an object **(E9)**

deposition [dep′ə•zish′ən] The process of dropping, or depositing, sediment in a new location **(C7)**

desalination [dē•sal′ə•nā′shən] The process of removing salt from sea water **(C120)**

diffusion [di•fyōō′zhən] The process by which many materials move in and out of cells **(A10)**

direct development [də•rekt′ di•vel′əp•mənt] A kind of growth where organisms keep the same body features as they grow larger **(A72)**

dominant trait [dom′ə•nənt trāt′] A strong trait **(A79)**

earthquake [ûrth′kwāk′] A shaking of the ground caused by the sudden release of energy in Earth's crust **(C18)**

eclipse [i•klips′] The passing of one object through the shadow of another **(D8)**

ecosystem [ek′ō•sis′təm] A community and its physical environment together **(B28)**

electric charge [i•lek′trik chärj′] The charge obtained by an object when it gains or loses electrons **(F68)**

electric circuit [i•lek′trik sûr′kit] The path along which electrons can flow **(F71)**

electric current [i•lek′trik kûr′ənt] The flow of electrons from negatively charged objects to positively charged objects **(F69)**

electric force [i•lek′trik fôrs′] The attraction or repulsion of objects due to their charges **(F69)**

electromagnet [i•lek′trō•mag′nit] A temporary magnet made by passing electric current through a wire coiled around an iron bar **(F72)**

electron [ē•lek′tron′] A subatomic particle with a negative charge **(E39)**

element [el′ə•mənt] A substance made up of only one kind of atom **(E40)**

El Niño [el nēn′yō] A short-term climate change that occurs every two to ten years **(C83)**

endangered [en•dān′jərd] A term describing a population of organisms that is likely to become extinct if steps are not taken to save it **(B51)**

energy [en′ər•jē] The ability to cause changes in matter **(F62)**

energy pyramid [en′ər•jē pir′ə•mid] Shows the amount of energy available to pass from one level of a food chain to the next **(B38)**

equinox [ē′kwi•noks] Point in Earth's orbit at which the hours of daylight and darkness are equal **(D15)**

erosion [i•rō′zhən] The process of moving sediment from one place to another **(C7)**

estuary [es′chōō•er′ē] The place where a freshwater river empties into an ocean **(B80, C102)**

evaporation [ē•vap′ə•rā′shən] The process by which a liquid changes into a gas **(B14, C67, E16)**

exotic [ig•zot′•ik] An imported or nonnative organism **(B50)**

extinct [ik•stingkt′] No longer in existence; describes a species when the last individual of a population dies and that organism is gone forever **(B51)**

fault [fôlt] A break or place where pieces of Earth's crust move **(C18)**

fiber [fi′bər] Any material that can be separated into threads **(A112)**

fish [fish] Vertebrates that live their entire life in water **(A44)**

food chain [fōōd′ chān′] The ways in which the organisms in an ecosystem interact with one another according to what they eat **(B35)**

food web [fōōd′ web′] Shows the interactions among many different food chains in a single ecosystem **(B36)**

force [fôrs] A push or pull that causes an object to move, stop, or change direction **(F6)**

fossil [fos′əl] The remains or traces of past life found in sedimentary rock **(C23)**

friction [frik′shən] A force that opposes, or acts against, motion when two surfaces rub against each other **(F6)**

front [frunt] The boundary between air masses **(C75)**

fungi [fun′jī′] Living things that look like plants but cannot make their own food; example, mushrooms **(A39)**

fusion energy [fyoo′zhən en′ər•jē] The energy released when the nuclei of two atoms are forced together to form a larger nucleus **(F112)**

galaxy [gal′ək•sē] A group of stars, gas, and dust **(D54)**

gas [gas] The state of matter that does not have a definite shape or volume **(E14)**

gene [jēn] Structures on a chromosome that contain the DNA code for a trait an organism inherits **(A80)**

genus [jē′nəs] The second-smallest name grouping used in classification **(A40)**

geothermal energy [jē′ō•thûr′məl en′ər•jē] Heat from inside the Earth **(F111)**

global warming [glō′bəl wôrm′ing] The hypothesized rise in Earth's average temperature from excess carbon dioxide **(C84)**

grain [grān] The seed of certain plants **(A110)**

gravitation [grav′i•tā′shən] The force that pulls all objects in the universe toward one another **(F8)**

greenhouse effect [grēn′hous′ i•fekt′] Process by which the Earth's atmosphere absorbs heat **(C84)**

gymnosperm [jim′nə•spûrm′] Plant with unprotected seeds; conifer or cone-bearing plant **(A102)**

habitat [hab′ə•tat′] A place in an ecosystem where a population lives **(B29)**

hardness [härd′nis] A mineral's ability to resist being scratched **(C37)**

headland [hed′land′] A hard, rocky point of land left when softer rock is washed away by the sea **(C111)**

heat [hēt] The transfer of thermal energy from one substance to another **(F84)**

humidity [hyoo•mid′ə•tē] A measure of the amount of water in the air **(C65)**

hydroelectric energy [hī′drō•ē•lek′trik en′ər•jē] Electricity generated from the force of moving water **(F104)**

igneous rock [ig′nē•əs rok′] A type of rock that forms when melted rock hardens **(C42)**

individual [in′də•vij′oo•əl] A single organism in an environment **(B28)**

inertia [in•ûr′shə] The property of matter that keeps it moving in a straight line or keeps it at rest **(F41)**

inherited trait [in•her′it•əd trāt′] A characteristic that is passed from parent to offspring **(A78)**

instinct [in′stingkt] A behavior that an organism inherits **(B46)**

insulator [in′sə•lāt′ər] A material that does not carry electrons **(F71)**

intertidal zone [in′tər•tīd′əl zōn′] An area where the tide and churning waves provide a constant supply of oxygen and nutrients to living organisms **(B77)**

invertebrates [in•vûr′tə•brits] Animals without a backbone **(A45)**

jetty [jet′ē] A wall-like structure made of rocks that sticks out into the ocean **(C112)**

joint [joint] A place where bones meet and are attached to each other and to muscles **(A24)**

kinetic energy [ki•net′ik en′ər•jē] The energy of motion, or energy in use **(F62)**

kingdom [king′dəm] The largest group into which living things can be classified **(A39)**

landform [land′fôrm′] A physical feature on Earth's surface **(C6)**

law of universal gravitation [lô′ uv yōōn′ə•vûr′səl grav′i•tā′shən] Law that states that all objects in the universe are attracted to all other objects **(F49)**

learned behavior [lûrnd′ bē•hāv′yər] A behavior an animal learns from its parents **(B46)**

lens [lenz] A piece of clear material that bends, or refracts, light rays passing through it **(F77)**

ligament [lig′ə•mənt] One of the bands of connective tissue that hold a skeleton together **(A25)**

light-year [līt′yir′] The distance light travels in one Earth year; about 9.5 trillion km **(D55)**

liquid [lik′wid] The state of matter that has a definite volume but no definite shape **(E14)**

local winds [lō′kəl windz′] The winds dependent upon local changes in temperature **(C73)**

luster [lus′tər] The way the surface of a mineral reflects light **(C37)**

machine [mə•shēn′] Something that makes work easier by changing the size or the direction of a force **(F20)**

magma [mag′mə] Hot, soft rock from Earth's lower mantle **(C16)**

magnetism [mag′nə•tiz′əm] The force of repulsion (pushing) or attraction (pulling) between poles of magnets **(F7)**

magnitude [mag′nə•tōōd] Brightness of stars **(D46)**

main sequence [mān′ sē′kwəns] A band of stars that includes most stars of average color, size, magnitude, and temperature **(D47)**

mammals [mam′əlz] Animals that have hair and produce milk for their young **(A44)**

mantle [man′təl] The layer of rock beneath Earth's crust **(C14)**

mass [mas] The amount of matter in an object **(E7)**

mass movement [mas′ mōōv′mənt] The downhill movement of rock and soil because of gravity **(C9)**

matter [mat′ər] Anything that has mass and takes up space **(E6)**

meiosis [mī•ō′sis] The process that reduces the number of chromosomes in reproductive cells **(A68)**

metamorphic rock [met′ə•môr′fik rok′] A type of rock changed by heat or pressure but not completely melted **(C46)**

metamorphosis [met′ə•môr′fə•sis] A change in the shape or characteristics of an organism's body as it grows **(A73)**

microclimate [mī′krō•klī′mit] The climate of a very small area **(C80)**

mineral [min′ər•əl] A natural, solid material with particles arranged in a repeating pattern **(C36)**

mitosis [mī•tō′sis] The process of cell division **(A65)**

molecule [mol′ə•kyōōl′] A grouping of two or more atoms joined together **(E40)**

moneran [mō•ner′ən] The kingdom of classification for organisms that have only one cell and no nucleus **(A39)**

momentum [mō•men′təm] A measure of how hard it is to slow down or stop an object **(F36)**

near-shore zone [nir′shôr′ zōn′] The area beyond the breaking waves that extends to waters that are about 180 m deep **(B77)**

nephrons [nef′ronz′] Tubes inside the kidneys where urea and water diffuse from the blood **(A20)**

net force [net′ fôrs′] The result of two or more forces acting together on an object **(F14)**

neuron [nŏŏr′on′] A specialized cell that can receive information and transmit it to other cells **(A26)**

neutron [nŏŏ′tron′] A subatomic particle with no charge **(E39)**

niche [nich] The role each population has in its habitat **(B29)**

nitrogen cycle [nī′trə•jən sī′kəl] The cycle in which nitrogen gas is changed into forms of nitrogen that plants can use **(B7)**

nonvascular plants [non•vas′kyə•lər plants] Plants that do not have tubes **(A52)**

nuclear energy [nŏŏ′klē•ər en′ər•jē] The energy released when the nucleus of an atom is split apart **(F110)**

nucleus [nŏŏ′klē•əs] **1** *(cell)* The organelle that controls all of a cell's activities **2** *(atom)* The center of an atom **(A8, E39)**

open-ocean zone [ō′pən•ō′shən zōn′] The area that includes most deep ocean waters; most organisms live near the surface **(B77)**

orbit [ôr′bit] The path one body in space takes as it revolves around another body; such as that of Earth as it revolves around the sun **(D7, F48)**

organ [ôr′gən] Tissues that work together to perform a specific function **(A12)**

osmosis [os•mō′sis] The diffusion of water and dissolved materials through cell membranes **(A10)**

Pangea [pan•jē′ə] A supercontinent containing all of Earth's land that existed about 225 million years ago **(C22)**

periodic table [pir′ē•od′ik tā′bəl] The table of elements in order of increasing atomic number; grouped by similar properties **(E47)**

phloem [flō′em] The tubes that transport food in the vascular plants **(A95)**

photosphere [fōt′ə•sfir′] The visible surface of the sun **(D41)**

photosynthesis [fōt′ō•sin′thə•sis] The process by which plants make food **(A96)**

physical properties [fiz′i•kəl prop′ər•tēz] The characteristics of a substance that can be observed or measured without changing the substance **(E6)**

pioneer plants [pī′ə•nir′ plantz′] The first plants to invade a bare area **(B92)**

pitch [pich] An element of sound determined by the speed at which sound waves move **(F79)**

planets [plan′its] Large, round bodies that revolve around a star **(D16)**

plate [plāt] A rigid block of crust and upper mantle rock **(C15)**

pollen [pol′ən] Flower structures that contain the male reproductive cells **(A102)**

pollution [pə•lōō′shən] Waste products that damage an ecosystem **(B99)**

population [pop•yə•lā′shən] All the individuals of the same kind living in the same environment **(B28)**

position [pə•zish′ən] An object's place, or location **(F34)**

potential energy [pō•ten′shəl en′ər•jē] The energy an object has because of its place or its condition **(F62)**

power [pou′ər] The amount of work done for each unit of time **(F19)**

precipitation [pri•sip′ə•tā′shən] Any form of water that falls from clouds, such as rain or snow **(B15, C65)**

prevailing winds [prē•vāl′ing windz′] The global winds that blow constantly from the same direction **(C73)**

producer [prə•dōōs′ər] An organism that makes its own food **(B34)**

protist [prō′tist] The kingdom of classification for organisms that have only one cell and also have a nucleus, or cell control center **(A39)**

proton [prō′ton′] A subatomic particle with a positive charge **(E39)**

radiation [rā′dē•ā′shən] The transfer of thermal energy by electromagnetic waves **(F85)**

reaction force [rē•ak′shən fôrs′] The force that pushes or pulls back in the third law of motion **(F43)**

reactivity [rē′ak•tiv′ə•tē] The ability of a substance to go through a chemical change **(E23)**

receptors [ri•sep′tərz] Nerve cells that detect conditions in the body's environment **(A26)**

recessive trait [ri•ses′iv trāt′] A weak trait **(A79)**

reclamation [rek′lə•mā′shən] The process of restoring a damaged ecosystem **(B110)**

recycle [rē•sī′kəl] To recover a resource from an item and use the recovered resource to make a new item **(B105)**

reduce [ri•dōōs′] To cut down on the use of resources **(B104)**

reflection [ri•flek′shən] The light energy that bounces off objects **(F76)**

refraction [ri•frak′shən] The bending of light rays when they pass through a substance **(F76)**

reptiles [rep′tīlz] Animals that have dry, scaly skin **(A44)**

resistor [ri•zis′tər] A material that resists the flow of electrons in some way **(F71)**

respiration [res′pə•rā′shən] The process that releases energy from food **(B8)**

reuse [rē′yo͞oz′] To use items again, sometimes for a different purpose **(B105)**

revolve [ri•volv′] To travel in a closed path around an object such as Earth does as it moves around the sun **(D6)**

rock [rok] A material made up of one or more minerals **(C42)**

rock cycle [rok′ si′kəl] The slow, never-ending process of rock changes **(C52)**

rotate [rō′tāt] The spinning of Earth on its axis **(D7)**

S

salinity [sə•lin′ə•tē] Saltiness of the ocean **(C97)**

satellite [sat′ə•līt′] A natural body, like the moon, or an artificial object that orbits another object **(D23)**

scuba [sko͞o′bə] Underwater breathing equipment; the letters stand for **s**elf-**c**ontained **u**nderwater **b**reathing **a**pparatus **(C117)**

sedimentary rock [sed′ə•men′tər•ē rok′] A type of rock formed by layers of sediments that were squeezed and stuck together over a long time **(C44)**

sexual reproduction [sek′sho͞o•əl rē′prə•duk′shən] The form of reproduction in which cells from two parents unite to form a zygote **(A68)**

shore [shôr] The area where the ocean and land meet and interact **(C110)**

solar energy [sō′lər en′ər•jē] The energy of sunlight **(F111)**

solar flare [sō′lər flâr′] A brief burst of energy from the sun's photosphere **(D42)**

solar wind [sō′lər wind′] A fast-moving stream of particles thrown into space by solar flares **(D42)**

solid [sol′id] The state of matter that has a definite shape and a definite volume **(E14)**

solstice [sol′stis] Point in Earth's orbit at which the hours of daylight are at their greatest or fewest **(D15)**

solubility [sol′yə•bil′ə•tē] The ability of one substance to be dissolved in another substance **(E10)**

sonar [sō′när′] A device that uses sound waves to determine water depth **(C117)**

space probe [spās′ prōb′] A robot vehicle used to explore deep space **(D24)**

species [spē′shēz] The smallest name grouping used in classification **(A40)**

speed [spēd] A measure of the distance an object moves in a given amount of time **(F35)**

spore [spôr] A single reproductive cell that grows into a new plant **(A101)**

streak [strēk] The color of the powder left behind when you rub a material against a white tile called a streak plate **(C37)**

submersible [sub•mûr′sə•bəl] An underwater vehicle **(C117)**

succession [sək•sesh′ən] A gradual change in an ecosystem, sometimes occurring over hundreds of years **(B92)**

sunspot [sun′spot′] A dark spot on the photosphere of the sun **(D42)**

symbiosis [sim′bē•ō′sis] A long-term relationship between different kinds of organisms **(B45)**

system [sis′təm] Organs that work together to perform a function **(A12)**

telescope [tel′ə•skōp′] An instrument that magnifies distant objects, or makes them appear larger (**D23**)

temperature [tem′pər•ə•chər] The average kinetic energy of all the molecules in an object (**F84**)

tendons [ten′dənz] Tough bands of connective tissue that attach muscles to bones (**A25**)

threatened [thret′ənd] Describes a population of organisms that are likely to become endangered if they are not protected (**B51**)

tidal energy [tīd′əl en′ər•jē] A form of hydroelectric energy that produces electricity from the rising and falling of tides (**F106**)

tide [tīd] The repeated rise and fall in the level of the ocean (**C106**)

tide pool [tīd′ pōōl′] A pool of sea water found along a rocky shoreline (**C111**)

tissue [tish′ōō] Cells that work together to perform a specific function (**A12**)

transpiration [tran′spə•rā′shən] The process in which plants give off water through their stomata (**B15**)

unbalanced forces [un•bal′ənst fôrs′əz] Forces that are not equal (**F13**)

universe [yōōn′ə•vûrs′] Everything that exists—planets, stars, dust, gases, and energy (**D54**)

vascular plants [vas′kyə•lər plants] Plants that have tubes (**A50**)

velocity [və•los′ə•tē] An object's speed in a particular direction (**F35**)

vertebrates [vûr′tə•brits] Animals with a backbone (**A44**)

villi [vil′ī] Projections sticking into the small intestine (**A19**)

volcano [vol•kā′nō] A mountain formed by lava and ash (**C16**)

volume [vol′yōōm] **1** *(measurement)* The amount of space that an object takes up **2** *(sound)* The loudness of a sound (**E8, F79**)

water cycle [wôt′ər sī′kəl] The cycle in which Earth's water moves through the environment (**B14**)

water pressure [wôt′ər presh′ər] The weight of water pressing on an object (**C97**)

wave [wāv] An up-and-down movement of surface water (**C102**)

weathering [weth′ər•ing] The process of breaking rock into soil, sand, and other tiny pieces (**C7**)

weight [wāt] A measure of the pull of gravity on an object (**E7**)

wetlands [wet′landz′] The water ecosystems that include saltwater marshes, mangrove swamps, and mud flats (**B111**)

work [wûrk] The use of a force to move an object through a distance (**F18**)

xylem [zī′ləm] The tubes that transport water and minerals in vascular plants (**A95**)

A

Abdominal muscles, R26
Absolute magnitude of stars, D46
Acceleration, F35
Acetabular cup, A83
Acid rain, B99, B117
Action force, F43
Activity pyramid, R12
Adaptations, A31, B43, B85
Adrenal glands, R37
Aeronautical engineer, F53
Agricultural scientists, A114–115
Agriculture, saltwater, C122–123
Agronomist, A115, C123, F114–115
Air, water in (chart), B15
Air mass, C75
Air pressure, C66, C89
Air tubes, R32
Algal blooms, B98
Allen, Joe, F24
Alloys, E43
Alpha International Space Station, D26
al-Razi, E50
Aluminum, E41
Alveoli, A18, R32
Alvin submersible, C117–119
Ammonia, B7
Amphibians, A44
Anemometer, C65
Angiosperms, A103
Animals
    with backbones, A44–45, A57
    without backbones, A45–47
    behavior of, B46
    body color of, B40–41
    cells of, A8–9
    diet of, B57
    kingdom of, A39–40
    life cycles of, A72–76, A106–107
    names for, A54–55
Anvil, F79, R22

Apollo 11, D29
Apollo astronauts, D24–25
Apollo program, D23, D29
Apparent magnitude, D46
Aqua-lung, C117
Aristotle, A54–55, C86, E38, E50, F40
Arizona Fish and Game Commission, B18–19
Armstrong, Neil, D29
Arp, Alissa J., B84
Arteries, A17–18, R30
Arthropods, A45
Asexual reproduction, A67
Ash, volcanic, C16
Asphalt, E28–29
Asteroids, D16–18
Astrolabe, D61
Astronauts, A30, D24–25, D29–30, F24–25, F54
Astronomer, D60
Astrophysicist, D59
Atmosphere, C64
Atmospheric conditions, C65
Atomic number, E40
Atomic theory, E38–39
Atoms, E38–40. *See also* Elements
Atrium, R31
Auditory canals, R22
Auditory nerves, R22
Auto mechanic, F115
Autonomic nervous system, R35
Axis, Earth's, D7

B

Backbones of animals, A42–47, A57
Bacteria (chart), B7
    in food, R10
Balanced forces, F12
Balances, R4
Bald eagles, B52, B114
Ballard, Robert D., C124
Baptist, Kia K., C28
Barometer, C65
Basalt, C43
Bay of Fundy tides (chart), C106

Beaches, C108–113
Beakers, R5
Behavior, animal, B46
Bell, Alexander Graham, F89
Bennett, Jean M., F90
Biceps, R26
Bicycling, R17
Bile duct, R28
Biomass, F110
Biomes. *See* Land biomes
Birds, A45. *See also* Animals
Bjerknes, Jacob, C86–87
Bladder, A20
Bleeding, first aid for, R21
Blood, R31
Blood vessels
    in circulatory system, A16, R30
    in respiratory system, R32–33
Bohr, Niels, E39
Boiling points, E18
Bone marrow, A24, R36
Bones, A24–25, R24–25, R27
Botanists, A56, A116
Boyko, Elisabeth, C122
Boyko, Hugo, C122
Boyle, Robert, E50
Bracken fern, A56
Brackish water ecosystems, B76, B80–81
Brain, A26, F91, R34
Breastbone, R24
Brock microscopes, R3
Bronchi, A18
Budding, A67
Butterfly Pavilion and Insect Center, CO, A120

C

Calcite mineral, C36
Calendars, D31
California condors, B52–53
Camouflage, B40–41, B42
Canola oil, F114–115
Canopy, B66–67, B70
Cantu, Eduardo S., A84
Cape Hatteras Lighthouse, C112

INDEX

Middle ear, R22
Milky Way Galaxy, D52–57
Minerals
    evaporation and, C57
    in oceans, C120
    properties of, C36–37
    uses for, C38–39
Mir Space Station, D29
Mission specialists, F25
Mitochondria, A9
Mitosis, A65–67
Mixtures, E10–11, E25, E31
Mohs' hardness scale, C37
Molecules, E40
Mollusks, A45
Molting, A73
Momentum
    conservation of, F44
    definition of, F36
Monerans, A39
Montreal Protocol, B115
Moon
    calendar and, D31
    eclipses and, D8
    exploring, D24–25
    orbit of, F48–51
    in space, D6–7
    surface of, D9
    tides and, C106
Morse, Samuel F. B., F89
Mosses, A52
Motion
    acceleration and, F35
    momentum and, F36–37, F44
    Newton's laws of, F40–43
    position and, F34
    speed of, F35
Mountains, C16
Mountain zone (chart), C82
Mount St. Helens, WA, B94–95,
    C16
Mouth
    in digestive system, R28
    in respiratory system, R32
Mucous membranes, nose, R23
Mudslides, C9
Mukai, Chiaki, F24
Muscular system, A22–23, A25,
    A46, R26–27

Musical instruments, F88
Mutualism, B45

N

Narrative writing, xxi
Nasal bones, R23
Nasal cavity, R23
National Aeronautics and Space
    Administration (NASA), D28
National Air and Space Muse-
    um, Washington, D.C., D64
National Audubon Society, B20
National Science Center,
    GA, F120
National Weather Service
    (NWS), C86, C128
National Zoo, Washington
    D. C., B55
Natural cycles, B6–11
*Natural History and Antiquities
    of Selborne, The* (White), B114
Natural succession, B92–95
Nautile, C118–119
Navarro, Julio, D60
Near-shore zone, B76, B77
Nebulae, D48, D56–57
Nephrons, A20
Neptune, D16–18
Nerves, R34
Nervous system, A12, A26,
    R34–35
Net force, F14
Neurons, A26–27, R34
Neutral atoms, E39
Neutral Buoyancy Laboratory
    (NBL), F24–25
Neutrons, E39, E51
Newton, Sir Isaac, D22–23,
    F40–43, F49, F51
Niches, B29
Nitrates, B7
Nitrogen cycle, B7
NMR spectroscopy, E30
Nodules, plant roots (chart), B7
Nonvascular plants, A52,
    A98–99, A100–101

Nose, R23, R32
Nostril, R23
Nuclear energy, F110
Nuclear physicist, E52
Nucleus
    of atoms, E39
    of cells, A8–9, A65 (chart)
Numbers, how scientists use,
    xxii–xxiii
Number sense, xxiii
Nutrients, A17
Nutrition, R8–11

O

Observing, x, xiv
Obsidian, C43
Oceans
    currents in, C104–105
    exploring, C26–27, C116–119
    food chains in, B82–83
    resources of, C120–121
    shorelines of, C108–113
    tides of, C106–107
    waves in, C102–103
    zones of, B76–77
Oil spills, F117
Olfactory bulb, R23
Olfactory tract, R23
Omnivores, B35
Open-ocean zone, B77
Optic nerves, R22
Orangutans, B55
Orbitals, atomic (chart), E39
Orbits
    of Earth's moon, D7
    of planets, F48–51
Order, A40
Oregon Dunes National
    Recreation Area, OR, B120
Organelles, A8
Organic chemists, C55
Organisms, communities of,
    B28
Organs, A12–13. *See also*
    Human body systems
Osmosis, A10–11
Outer ear, R22

Receptors, A26

Recessive traits, A79

Reclamation, B110

Recording data, xv

Recycle resources, B104, B105

Recycling Act of 1976, B115

Red giants, D47–49

Reduce resource use, B104–105

Reflected light, F74–75

Reflection, F76

Reflexes, A26–27

Refraction, F76

Regeneration, A66–67

Remote Manipulator System (RMS), F25

Reproduction

asexual, A67

in cells, A62–63

in cone-bearing vascular plants, A102

in flowering vascular plants, A103–105

life cycles and, A106–107

in nonvascular plants, A100–101

sexual, A68

in simple vascular plants, A101

Reptiles, A44. *See also* Animals

Resistors, F71

Resonance, F80

Resources

competition for, B42–43

ocean, C120–121

sharing, B43–44

symbiosis and, B45

using, B104–107

Respiration, B8

Respiratory system, A18, R32–33

Restoring ecosystems, B110–113, B117

Retina, R22

Reuse of natural materials

balance in, B10–11

carbon-oxygen cycle in, B8–9

nitrogen cycle in, B7

Reuse resources, B104–105

Revolution (Earth-moon system), D6–7

Revolve, D6

Rib cage, R24–25

Rip currents, C104

Rivers, B15, B110

Rocket-based combined cycle (RBCC) engine, F52–53

Rockets, D28–29, F55

Rock cycle, C48–49, C52–53

Rocks

changes in, C50–51

igneous, C42–43

metamorphic, C46

records in, C23. *See also* Earth

sedimentary, C44–45

weathering of, C57

Rogue waves, C103

Root hairs, A93

Roots, plant, A92–94

Roots of words, R46–47

Rotate, D7

Rotation, Earth's, D7

Ruffini's endings, R23

Runoff, C67

Russell, Henry, D47

Russell, James T., F89

RXTE satellite, D50

S

Safety, xxiv, R10–11, R18–21

Salinity, C97

Saliva, A19

Salivary glands, R29

Salt water (chart), B14

Saltwater agriculture, C122–123

Saltwater ecosystems, B76, B77

San Andreas fault, CA, C15

Sand spits, C110

Sandstone, C45

Sapwood, A51

Satellite images, C26–27

Satellites, D23, D50

Satellite technician, C27

Saturn, D16–18

Scales, on conifers, A102

Scanning tunneling microscope, E51

Scavengers, B39

Sceptical Chymist, The (Boyle), E50

Schist, C46

Schmitt, Harrison, D30

Science reading strategies, R38–43

Science tools, R2–5

Science vocabulary, R44–49

Scientific methods, x–xii

Scientists, how they work, x–xxiv

Screw, F22

Scuba, C117

Sea-viewing Wide Field Sensor (Sea-WiFS), B82–83

Secondary succession, B94–95

Sediment, C7

Sedimentary rocks, C44–45, C52–53

Seedlings, A105

Seeds, A104–107

Seismic waves, C18

Seismograph, C18

Self-healing asphalt, E28–29

Semicircular canals, R22

Sense organs, R22–23

Series circuit (chart), F70

Serving size, R9

Sexual reproduction, A68

Shellfish, B80

Shield volcanoes (chart), C17

Shoreline currents, C104

Shores, C108–113

Show Low wetland, AZ, B18–19

Sight, R22

Silent Spring (Carson), B114–115

Silicon, E41

Siltstone, C44

Silver, C38

Simple vascular plants, A101

Sinkholes, C9

Skeletal system, A25, A31, A47, R24–25, R27

Skin, A7, R23

Slate, C46

Small intestine, R28

Smell, R23

Smooth muscles, A25

U

U.S. Army Tank Automotive Command (TACOM), B56
U.S. Forest Service (USFS), B18–19
Ulna bone, R24
Unbalanced forces, F13
Undersea explorers, C124
Universe, D54
Universal gravitation, F49
Updrafts, C73
Uranus, D16–18
Ureters, A20
Urethra, A20

V

Vaccines, A28–29
Vacuoles, A9
Valley glaciers, C8
Van de Graaff generator, F66
Vascular plants
    leaves of, A92, A96
    parts of, A50–51
    reproduction in, A101–107
    roots of, A92–94
    stems of, A92, A94–95
Veins, A17–18, R30
Velocity, F35, F38–39
Ventricles, R31
Venus, D16–18
Vertebrae, R25
Vertebrates, A44–45. *See also* Animals
Very Large Array radio telescopes, NM, D50
Veterinary technicians, A83
Viking program, D24
Villi, A19
Volcanoes, C10, C16–17
Volume, E8, F79
Voluntary muscles, A25
Voyager program, D24

W

Walking, R17
Warm-up stretches, R14–15
War of 1812, D28
Washers, F22
Wastewater, B108–109
Water
    adult human daily use of (chart), A20
    cycle of, C67
    on Earth versus moon, D10
    ecosystems of. *See* Water ecosystems
    humans and, B16–17
    landforms changed by, C7
    in plants, A117
Water cycle, B12–17, B21, C67
Water ecosystems
    estuaries, B80–81
    freshwater, B76, B78–79
    interactions in, B85
    saltwater, B76–77
Water pressure, C97
Water vapor, C67–69
Waves
    electromagnetic, F78
    ocean, C102–103
    sound, F79–80, F91
Weather
    air pressure and, C66
    forecasting, C86–87
    measuring, C65
    occurrence of, C64
    sun and, C72
    water and, C67–69
    winds and, C73–75
    See also Climate; Water cycle
Weathering, C7, C50, D10
Wedge, F20
Weight, E7
Weightlessness, F24–25
Westerlies, C74

Wetlands, B18–19, B110–111
Wheel and axle, F21–22
White, Gilbert, B114–115
White blood cells, R36
White dwarf stars, D48
Windpipe, A18, R32
Wind
    landforms changed by, C8
    prevailing, C73–75
    waves and, C102–103
Wind vane, C65
Wood, A112
Woodchucks, A54
Woolly mammoths, C24
Work
    calculating, F19
    effort in, F18
    machines and, F20–22
    measurement of, F16–17
    weightless, F24–25
Working out, R13
World climates, C82
Wrist, R25
Writing, how scientists use, xxi

X

Xylem, A95

Y

Yellowstone National Park, B94–95, B115

Z

Zoo guides, B55
Zooplankton, B82–83
Zoos, B54–55
Zworykin, Vladimir, F89
Zygotes
    in reproduction, A68, A101–102

Page Placement Key:
(l)-left, (r)-right, (t)-top, (c)-center, (b)-bottom, (bg)-background, (fg)-foreground, (i)-inset

Cover and Title Pages
Wolfgang Kaehler/Corbis; (bg) Eduardo Garcia/FPG International

Table of Contents
iv (t) Anup & Manoj Shah/Animals Animals; iv (bg) Grant V. Faint/The Image Bank; v (t) Zig Leszczynski/Animals Animals; v (bg) Karl Hentz/The Image Bank; vi (t) Eric & David Hosking/Photo Researchers; vi (bg) Bios (Klein-Hubert)/Peter Arnold, Inc; vii Telegraph Colour Library/FPG International; viii (t) Alvis Upitis/The Image Bank; viii (bg) Tim Crosby/Liaison International; ix (t) David Zaitz/Photonica; ix (bg) Stone;

Unit A
Unit A Opener (fg) Anup & Manoj Shah/Animals Animals; (bg)Grant V. Faint/The Image Bank; A2-A3 Image Shop/Phototake; A3 (l) Lawrence Migdale/Photo Researchers; A3 (c) Quest/Science Photo Library/Photo Researchers; A4 Charles D. Winters/Timeframe Photography, Inc./Photo Researchers; A6 (l) The Granger Collection, New York; A6 (c), (r) Courtesy of Hunt Institute for Botanical Documentation, Carnegie Mellon University, Pittsburgh, PA; A7 (tl) Ed Reschke/Peter Arnold, Inc.; A7 (tr) Michel Viard/Peter Arnold, Inc.; A7 (bl) Courtesy of Dr. Sam Harbo D.V.M., and Dr. Jurgen Schumacher D.V.M. , Veterinary Hospital, University of Tennessee; A7 (br) A.B. Sheldon/Dembinsky Photo Associates; A8 Dwight R. Kuhn; A9 Courtesy of Dr. Sam Harbo D.V.M., and Dr. Jurgen Schumacher D.V.M., Veterinary Hospital, University of Tennessee; A11 Skip Moody/Dembinsky Photo Associates; A14 Michael Newman/PhotoEdit; A16 (l) Dr. Tony Brain/Science Photo Library/Photo Researchers; A16 (r) Prof. P. Motta/Dept. of Anatomy/University "La Sapienza", Rome/Science Photo Library/Photo Researchers; A22 Gary Holscher/Stone; A28 D. Cavagnaro/DRK; A28 (i) Dr. Dennis Kunkel/Phototake; A29 Mark Richards/PhotoEdit; A30 NASA; A33 Charles D. Winters/Timeframe Photography, Inc./Photo Researchers; A34-A35 Gregory Ochocki/Photo Researchers; A35 (t) Dave Watts/Tom Stack & Associates; A35 (b) Frances Fawcett/Cornell University/American Indian Program; A36 Christian Grzimek/Okapia/Photo Reseachers; A38-A39 Bill Lea/Dembinsky Photo Associates; A38 (l) MESZA/Bruce Coleman, Inc.; A38 (c) Andrew Syred/SPL/Photo Researchers; A38 (r) Robert Brons/BPS/Stone; A39 (t) Bill Lea/Dembinsky Photo Associates; A39 (tc) Dr. E. R. Degginger/Color-Pic; A39 (c) S. Nielsen/Bruce Coleman, Inc.; A39 (bc) Robert Brons/BPS/Stone; A39 (b) Andrew Syred/SPL/Photo Researchers; A41 Daniel Cox/Stone; A42 Arthur C. Smith, III/Grant Heilman Photography; A44 (t) Ana Laura Gonzalez/Animals Animals; A44 (b) Tom Brakefield/The Stock Market; A44-A45 Runk/Schoenberger/Grant Heilman Photography; A45 (tl) Amos Nachoum/The Stock Market; A45 (tc) Hans Pfletschinger/Peter Arnold, Inc.; A45 (tr) Mark Moffett/Minden Pictures; A45 (br) Larry Lipsky/DRK; A46 (t) James Balog/Stone; A46 (b) Stephen Dalton/Photo Researchers; A48 Darrell Gulin/Stone; A50 Dr. E. R. Degginger, FPSA/Color-Pic; A51 Phil A. Dotson/Photo Researchers; A52 (t) Heather Angel/Biofotos; A52 (c) Runk Schoenberger/Grant Heilman Photography; A52-A53 Runk Schoenberger/Grant Heilman Photography; A54 Leonard Lee Rue III/Photo Researchers; A54-A55 S. J. Krasemann/Peter Arnold, Inc.; A55 (tl) Art Resource, NY; A55 (tr) Dr. E. R. Degginger/Photo Researchers; A55 (bl) Superstock; A55 (br) The Granger Collection, New York; A56 (t) Courtesy of Hunt Institute for Botanical Documentation, Carnegie Mellon University, Pittsburg, PA; A56 (b) Grant Heilman Photography; A60-A61 Rob & Ann Simpson/Visuals Unlimited; A61 (l) Dwight R. Kuhn; A61 (r) Dr. D. Spector/Peter Arnold, Inc.; A62 Ron Kimball; A64 (l) Jerome Wexler/Photo Researchers; A64 (cl), (c) Carolina Biological Supply Company/Phototake; A64 (cr) Jerome Wexler/Photo Researchers; A64 (r) Kenneth H. Thomas/Photo Researchers; A65 Conly L. Rieder/BPS/Stone; A66 (tl), (tc), (tr) Carolina Biological Supply Company/Phototake; A66 (c) Noble Proctor/Photo Researchers; A66 (b) Zig Leszczynski/Animals Animals; A67 (tl), (tc), (tr) Carolina Biological Supply Company/Phototake; A67 (b) Bob Gossington/Bruce Coleman, Inc.; A69 Carolina Biological Supply Company/Phototake; A70 J.H. Robinson/Photo Researchers; A72 (t) Peter A. Simon/Phototake; A72 (b) Dr. E.R. Degginger/Photo Researchers; A73 (l) Thomas Gulz/Visuals Unlimited; A73 (c) Dwight R. Kuhn; A73 (r) William J. Weber/Visuals Unlimited; A74 Harry Rogers/Photo Researchers; A75 Michael Fogden/Bruce Coleman, Inc.; A76 Paul Barton/The Stock Market; A78 Phil Savoie/The Picture Cube; A79 The Granger Collection, New York; A82 Tim Davis/Tony Stone Images; A83 (li) College of Veterinary Medicine/University of Florida; A83 (r) Zigy Kaluzny/Tony Stone Images; A84 Henry Friedman/HRW; A84 (i) Oliver Meckes/Photo Researchers; A88-A89 Tom Bean/Stone; A89 (t) Inga Spence/Visuals Unlimited; A89 (b) Ned Therrien/Visuals Unlimited; A90 James Randklev/Stone; A92 (l) Richard Choy/Peter Arnold, Inc.; A92 (r) Reinhard Siegel/Stone; A93 Norman Myers/Bruce Coleman, Inc.; A93 (li) Dr. E. R. Degginger/Color-Pic; A93 (ri) John Kaprielian/Photo Researchers; A95 Jane Grushow/Grant Heilman Photography; A96-A97 (t), A96 (ti) Runk/Schoenberger/Grant Heilman Photography; A96-A97 (b) Alan Levenson/Stone; A98 Darrell Gulin/Dembinsky Photo Associates; A100 Kim Taylor/Bruce Coleman, Inc.; A101, A102 (t) Runk/Schoenberger/Grant Heilman Photography; A102 (b) S.J. Krasemann/Peter Arnold, Inc.; A103 (t) Dr. E. R. Degginger/Color-Pic; A103 (b) Robert Maier/Earth Scenes; A104 (t) David Cavagnaro/Peter Arnold, Inc.; A104 (tc) E. R. Degginger/Bruce Coleman, Inc.; A104 (bc) Gregory K. Scott/Photo Researchers; A104 (b) Kevin Schafer Photography; A104 (bg) Jeff Lepore/Photo Researchers; A105 Runk/Schoenberger/Grant Heilman Photography; A106 (animal life cycle) (t) Gregory K. Scott/Photo Researchers; A106 (r) Harry Rogers/National Audubon Society; A106 (b) David M. Dennis/Tom Stack & Associates; A106 (l) Jen & Des Bartlett/Bruce Coleman, Inc.; A106 (plant life cycle) (t) Dr. E. R. Degginger/Color-Pic; A106 (r) Barry L. Runk/Grant Heilman Photography; A106 (b) Jane Grushow/Grant Heilman Photography; A106 (l) Dwight R. Kuhn; A112 (l) Alan & Linda Detrick/Photo Researchers; A112 (cr) Angelina Lax/Photo Researchers; A113 Grant Heilman Photography; A113 (i) Will & Deni McIntyre/Photo Researchers; A114-115 Dana Downie/AGStock USA; A115 (b) Mark Richards/PhotoEdit; A116 Dennis Carlyle Darling/ HRW; A118 Dr. E. R. Degginger/Color-Pic; A119 James Randklev/Stone; A120 (t) Jeff Greenberg/Unicorn Stock Photos; A120 (b) Jack Olson Photography;

Unit B
Unit B Opener (fg) Zig Leszczynski/Animals Animals; (bg) Karl Hentz/The Image Bank; B2 Clyde H. Smith/Peter Arnold, Inc.; B2-B3 Superstock; B3 Earl Roberge/Photo Researchers; B4 Wolfgang Kaehler Photography; B6 Randy Ury/The Stock Market; B7 Thomas Hovland/Grant Heilman Photography; B10 Wolfgang Kaehler Photography; B12 Michael Giannechini/Photo Researchers; B14-B15 Greg Vaughn/Stone; B16 (t) C. Vincent/Natural Selection Stock Photography; B16 (b) Bob Daemmrich Photography, Inc.; B16 (bi) Superstock; B18 John Shaw/Bruce Coleman, Inc.; B18-B19 Lee Rentz/Bruce Coleman, Inc.; B19 Ken Graham/Bruce Coleman, Inc.; B20 Sipa Press; B22 Greg Vaughn/Stone; B23 C. Vincent/Natural Selection Stock Photography; B24-B25 P & R Hagan/Bruce Coleman, Inc.; B25 (t) Tomas del Amo/Pacific Stock; B25 (b) Mitsuaki Iwago/Minden Pictures; B26 Tim Davis/Photo Researchers; B28 (li) Michael Giannechini/Photo Researchers; B28-B29 (bg) J.A. Kravlis/Masterfile; B28-B29 (ci) Ted Kerasote/Photo Researchers; B29 (ti) Superstock; B29 (bi) Mitsuaki Iwago/Minden Pictures; B30 (tl) David Muench Photography, Inc.; B30 (tr), (bl) Barry L. Runk/Grant Heilman Photography; B30 (br) David Muench Photography, Inc.; B32 Superstock; B34 (tli) V.P. Weinland/Photo Researchers; B34 (tri) Parviz M. Pour/Photo Researchers; B34-B35 (bi) Dembinsky Photo Associates; B34-B35 (bg) Larry Ditto/Bruce Coleman, Inc.; B35 (li) Tom McHugh/Photo Researchers; B35 (ri) Tom & Pat Leeson/Photo Researchers; B36-B37 Woods, Michael J./NGS Image Collection; B39 Bruce Coleman, Inc.; B40 (both) Joe McDonald/McDonald Wildlife Photography; B42 (bg) Stuart Westmorland/Stone; B42 (li) Roger Bickel/New England Stock Photo; B42 (ri) Bruce Coleman, Inc.; B43 (l) Kevin Schafer/Peter Arnold, Inc.; B43 (r) Mitsuaki Iwago/Minden Pictures; B44 (t) John Shaw/Bruce Coleman, Inc.; B44 (c) Hal H. Harrison/Photo Researchers; B44 (b) Wayne Lankinen/Bruce Coleman, Inc.; B45 (t) M. & C. Photography/Peter Arnold, Inc.; B45 (b) William Townsend/Photo Researchers; B46 (t) Vince Streano/The Stock Market; B46-B47 Ralph Ginzburg/Peter Arnold, Inc.; B48 Bryan & Cherry Alexander/Masterfile; B50 (t) Tim Davis/Photo Researchers; B50 (bl) Johnny Johnson/Tony Stone Images; B50 (br) Malcolm Boulton/Photo Researchers; B51 Tom McHugh/Photo Researchers; B52-B53 Ted Schiffman/Peter Arnold, Inc; B52 Roy Toft/Tom Stack & Associates; B54 Gunter Ziesler/Peter Arnold, Inc.; B55 (t) Doug Cheeseman/Peter Arnold, Inc.; B55 (b) Bonnie Kamin/PhotoEdit; B56 (i) Louisiana State University Chemistry Library Website; B56 Meckes/Ottawa/Photo Researchers; B60-B61 Craig Tuttle/The Stock Market; B61 (t) Jake Rajs/Stone; B61 (b) Earth Satellite Corporation/Science Photo Library/Photo Researchers; B62 Chromosohm/Sohm/Stone; B64 (t) David Muench Photography, Inc.; B64 (b) Gary Braasch/Stone; B65 (tl) Superstock; B65 (tr) Steve Kaufman/Peter Arnold, Inc.; B65 (bl) Joseph Van Os/The Image Bank; B65 (br) Colin Prior/Stone; B66 Wolfgang Kaehler Photography; B66 (i) Mark Moffett/Minden Pictures; B67 Superstock; B67 (i) Roger Bickel/New England Stock Photo; B68 David Muench Photography, Inc.; B68 (i) William Manning/The Stock Market; B69 Darrell Gulin/Stone; B69 (i) T. Eggers/The Stock Market; B70 David Muench Photography, Inc.; B70 (i) Joseph Van Os/The Image Bank; B71 Carr Clifton/Minden Pictures; B71 (i) Kennan Ward Photography; B72 (l) Nicholas DeVore, III/Bruce Coleman, Inc.; B72 (r) Tui De Roy/Minden Pictures; B74 Stan Osolinski/The Stock Market; B80 (t) Jim Brandenburg/Minden Pictures; B80 (b) David Muench Photography, Inc.; B82 (t) © Corel; B82-B83 Manfred Kage/Peter Arnold; B83 (t) NASA GSFC/Science Photo Library/Photo Researchers; B83 (bi) Pete Saloutos/The Stock Market; B84 (t) Romberg Tiburon Center; B84 (b) Emory Kristof/NGS Image Collection; B86 Jim Bradenburg/Minden Pictures; B88-B89 Gary Brettnacher/Stone; B89 (t) Jonathan Wallen; B89 (b) Argus Fotoarchiv/Peter Arnold, Inc.; B90 Frans Lanting/Minden Pictures; B92 Runk/Schoenberger/Grant Heilman Photography; B93 (t) Kennan Ward Photography; B93 (b) Ed Reschke/Peter Arnold, Inc.; B94 (t) Larry Nielsen/Peter Arnold, Inc.; B94 (c) John Marshall/Stone; B94 (b) Jeff & Alexa Henry/Peter Arnold, Inc.; B96 Art Wolfe/Stone; B98 Mark E. Gibson; B98 (i) Dr. E.R. Degginger/Color-Pic; B99 J.H. Robinson/Photo Researchers; B100 Francois Gohier/Photo Researchers; B101 Tony Arruza/Bruce Coleman, Inc.; B104 (c) Jim Corwin/Stone; B106 Tim Davis/Photo Researchers; B110 Mark E. Gibson; B111 (l) Bernard Boutrit/Woodfin Camp & Associates; B111 (r) Bill Tiernan/The Virginian-Pilot; B112 Courtesy of Atlanta Botanical Gardens; B112 (i) Kenneth Murray/Photo Researchers; B114 John Hyde/Bruce Coleman, Inc.; B114 (tli) Superstock; B114 (tri) Tom Bean/The Stock Market; B116 Centre For Ecological Studies; B116 (i) E. Hanumantha/Photo Researchers; B120 (t) Bill M. Campbell, MD; B120 (b) Graeme Teague Photography;

Unit C
Unit C Opener (fg) Eric & David Hosking/Photo Researchers; (bg) Bios (Klein-Hubert)/Peter Arnold, Inc.; C2-C3 Roger Werth/Woodfin Camp & Associates; C3 (t) John Livzey/Stone; C3 (b) Royal Oservatory, Edinburgh/Science Photo Library/Photo Researchers; C4 Tom Bean/Tom & Susan Bean, Inc.; C6 (tl) Helen Paraskevas; C6 (tr) Tom Bean/Tom & Susan Bean, Inc.; C6 (bi) Mark E. Gibson; C6-C7 Eric Neurath/Stock, Boston; C7 (t) NASA Photo/Grant Heilman Photography; C7 (b) Digital Visual Library/US Army Corps of Engineers; C8 (both) Mark E. Gibson; C9 M.T. O'Keefe/Bruce Coleman, Inc.; C10-C11 Michael Collier/Stock, Boston; C12 Soames Summerhays/Photo Researchers; C16 G. Gualco/Bruce Coleman, Inc.; C17 (t) Gregory G. Dimijian/Photo Researchers; C17 (c) Krafft/Explorer/Science Source/Photo Researchers; C17 (b) Tom & Pat Leeson/Photo Researchers; C18 UPI/Corbis-Bettmann; C20 M.P.L. Fogden/Bruce Coleman, Inc.; C23 Tom Bean/Tom & Susan Bean, Inc.; C24 A. J. Copley/Visuals Unlimited; C25 (t) R.T. Nowitz/Photo Researchers; C26 NASA; C27 (t) Walter H. F. Smith & David T. Sandwell/NOAA National Data Centers; C27 (b) David Young-Wolff/PhotoEdit; C28 (i) Santa Fabio/Black Star/Harcourt; C28 Tom Bean/Tom & Susan Bean, Inc.; C31 (l) Dr. E. R. Degginger/Color-Pic; C31 (r) Joyce Photographics/Photo Researchers; C32-C33 Dan Suzio/Photo Researchers; C33 (tl) Sam Ogden/Science Photo Library/Photo Researchers; C33 (br) Breck P. Kent/Earth Scenes; C34 The Natural History Museum, London; C36 (tl) Dr. E.R. Degginger/Color-Pic; C36 (bl) E.R. Degginger/Bruce Coleman, Inc.; C36 (bc) Joy Spurr/Bruce Coleman, Inc.; C36 (br), (c1) Dr. E.R. Degginger/Color-Pic; C37 (c2), (c3) E.R. Degginger/Bruce Coleman, Inc.; C37 (c5), (c6), (c8) Dr. E.R. Degginger/Color-Pic; C37 (c9) Mark A. Schneider/Dembinsky Photo Associates; C37 (c10) Dr. E.R. Degginger/Bruce Coleman, Inc.; C38 (tl) Dr. E.R. Degginger/Color-Pic; C38 (cl) Biophoto Associates/Photo Researchers; C38 (cr) Andy Sacks/Stone; C38 (bl) Dr. E.R. Degginger/Color-Pic; C38 (br) B. Daemmrich/The Image Works; C40 Joe McDonald/Bruce Coleman, Inc.; C42 (t) Dr. E.R. Degginger/Color-Pic; C42 (b) Phillip Hayson/Photo Researchers; C43 (tl), (tcl) Dr. E.R. Degginger/Color-Pic; C43

(tcr) Breck P. Kent/Earth Scenes; C43 (tr) Robert Pettit/Dembinsky Photo Associates; C43 (b) Martha McBride/Unicorn Stock Photos; C44, C45 (tl), (tcl), (tcr), (tr) Dr. E.R. Degginger/Color-Pic; C45 (b) David Bassett/Stone; C46 (t) G. R. Roberts Photo Library; C46 (b), C46-C47, C47 Dr. E.R. Degginger/Color-Pic; C48 Tom Till/Auscape; C50, C51 (t), (b), C52 (l), (r), C52-C53 Dr. E.R. Degginger/Color-Pic; C54 James P. Blair & Victor Boswell/NGS Image Collection; C55 Mark Richards/Photo Edit; C56 Stuart McCall/Tony Stone Images; C56 (i) Photo Courtesy of Mrs. Alma G. Gipson; C60-C61 Bob Abraham/The Stock Market; C61 (t) NASA/The Stock Market; C61 (b) Stan Osolinski/The Stock Market; C62 (b) Warren Faidley/International Stock Photography; C64 (l) Everett Johnson/Stone; C64 (r) Warren Faidley/International Stock Photography; C65 (bg) Orion/International Stock Photography; C65 (bli) M. Antman/The Image Works; C65 (bri) Dr. E. R. Degginger/Color-Pic; C66 (t) David M. Grossman/Photo Researchers; C66 (b) Mark Stephenson/Westlight; C68 (l) Dan Sudia/Photo Researchers; C68 (tr) Kent Wood/Photo Researchers; C68 (cr) Kevin Schafer/Peter Arnold, Inc.; C68 (br) Gary Meszaros/Dembinsky Photo Associates; C74 Larry Mishkar/Dembinsky Photo Associates; C78 (b) Richard Brown/Stone; C80 (l) Tom Till; C80 (c) Blaine Harrington III/The Stock Market; C80 (r) Coco McCoy/Rainbow; C81 (t) Randy Ury/The Stock Market; C81 (c) Larry Cameron/Photo Researchers; C81 (b) Jeff Greenberg/Photo Researchers; C82 (l) Ron Sefton/Bruce Coleman, Inc.; C82 (cl) Fritz Prenzel/Peter Arnold, Inc.; C82 (c) John Lawrence/Stone; C82 (cr) Marcello Bertinetti/Photo Researchers; C82 (r) Jose Fuste Raga/The Stock Market; C83 Paul Sequeira/Photo Researchers; C83 (i) Joe Sohm/Chromosomm/Photo Researchers; C84-C85 J. Richardson/Westlight; C86 (l) Brad Gaber/The Stock Market; C86-C87 A. Ramey/Woodfin Camp & Associates; C87 (l) NASA; C87 (r) Phil Degginger/Bruce Coleman, Inc.; C88 NASA/Goddard Space Flight Center/Science Photo Library/Photo Researchers; C88 (i) Eli Reichman/HRW; C92-C93 RKO Radio Pictures/Archive Photos; C93 (t) Thomas Abercrombiengs/NGS Image Collection; C93 (b) Clyde H. Smith/Peter Arnold, Inc.; C94 Sylvia Stevens; C97 (t) Timothy O' Keefe/Bruce Coleman, Inc.; C97 (b) Joseph J. Scherschel/NGS Image Collection; C97 (i) Carlos Lacamara/NGS Image Collection; C100 George D. Lepp/Photo Researchers; C102 Vince Cavataio/Pacific Stock; C103 (t) The Stock Market; C103 (ti) Michael P. Gadomski/Bruce Coleman, Inc.; C103 (bl) UPI/Corbis-Bettmann; C103 (br) Chip Porter/AllStock/PNI; C104 (t) Tony Arruza/Bruce Coleman, Inc.; C104 (b) Dr. Richard Legeckis/Science Photo Library/Photo Researchers; C105 George Marler/Bruce Coleman, Inc.; C106 (l), (r) John Elk/Stock, Boston; C110 (l) Brian Parker/Tom Stack & Associates; C110 (r) S.L. Craig, Jr./Bruce Coleman, Inc.; C111 (l) William E. Ferguson; C111 (r) Toms & Susan Bean, Inc.; C112 (t) Bruce Roberts/Photo Researchers; C112 (c) William Johnson/Stock, Boston; C112 (b) Wendel Metzer/Bruce Coleman, Inc.; C112-C113 Bob Daemmrich/Stock, Boston; C114 Michael Paris Photography; C116 (t) The Granger Collection, New York; C116 (bl) Corbis-Bettmann; C116 (br) The Granger Collection, New York; C116-C117 Eric Le Norcy-Bios/Peter Arnold, Inc.; C117 (tl) Naval Undersea Museum; C117 (tr) NASA/Science Photo Library/Photo Researchers; C117 (bl) Courtesy Smithsonian Diving Office/Photograph by Diane L. Nordeck; C117 (br) James P. Blair/NGS Image Collection; C118 (t) Woods Hole Oceanographic Institution; C118 (bl), (br), C119 (t) Emory Kristof/NGS Image Collection; C119 (c) Culver Pictures; C119 (b) Woods Hole Oceanographic Institution; C120 Allen Green/Photo Researchers; C121 Christian Vioujard/Gamma Liaison; C122 (t) © PhotoDisc; C122 (b) Mike Price/Bruce Coleman, Inc.; C123 (t) Eric Freedman/Bruce Coleman, Inc.; C123 (b) David Woodfall/Stone; C124 Susan Lapides/Woodfin Camp & Associates; C124 (i) Emory Kristof/NGS Image Collection; C128 (t) Brownie Harris/The Stock Market; C128 (b) Adam Jones/Dembinsky Photo Associates;

Unit D

Unit D Opener (fg), (bg) Telegraph Colour Library/FPG International; D2-D3 Guodo Cozzi/Bruce Coleman, Inc.; D3 (l) Ray Pfortner/Peter Arnold, Inc.; D3 (r) Painting by Helmut Wimmer; D4 NASA; D6, D7 Frank Rossotto/StockTrek; D8 (t) Dennis Di Cico/Peter Arnold, Inc.; D8 (b) Frank Rossotto/StockTrek; D9, D10 (tr), (tl) NASA; D10 (ctl) Francois Gohier/Photo Researchers; D10 (ctr), (cbr) NASA; D10 (bl) Paul Stepan/Photo Researchers; D10 (br), D12 NASA; D14 (l) Peter Marbach; D14 (r) Jeff Greenberg/Unicorn Stock Photos; D15 Fred Habegger/Grant Heilman Photography; D18 NASA; D18 (Pluto) Dr. R. Albrecht, ESA/ESO Space Telescope European Coordinating Facility/NASA; D19 E. R. Degginger/Color-Pic; D20 NASA; D22 (t) The Granger Collection, New York; D22 (bl) Martha Cooper/Peter Arnold, Inc.; D22 (br) The Granger Collection, New York; D22, D23, D24 (bg) Science Photo Library/Photo Researchers; D23 (tl) Sovfoto/Eastfoto; D23 (tr) NASA; D23 (bl) Courtesy of AT&T Archives; D23 (br),D24, D25, D26-D27, D28, D29, D30, D33 NASA; D34-D35 Jerry Schad/Photo Researchers; D35 NASA; D36 StockTrek; D39 (t) Warren Faidley/International Stock Photography; D39 (c) Pekka Parviainen/Science Photo Library/Photo Researchers; D39 (b) Brian Atkinson/Stone; D40 (t) Rev. Ronald Royer/Science Photo Library/Photo Researchers; D40 (c) NASA; D40 (b) Hale Observatory/SS/Photo Researchers; D42 Wards Sci/Science Source/Photo Researchers; D46 John Chumack/Photo Researchers; D48 Andrea Dupree (Harvard-Smithsonian CfA), Ronald Gilliland (STScI), NASA and ESA; D49 Jeff Hester and Paul Scowen (Arizona State University), and NASA; D50 (l) NASA; D50 (r) Roger Ressmeyer/Corbis; D50 (b) Francois Gohier/Photo Researchers; D52 Bill Ross/Stone; D54 Fred Espenak/Science Photo Library/Photo Researchers; D55 Lynette Cook/Science Photo Library/Photo Researchers; D56 (t) Royal Observatory, Edinburgh/AATB/Science Photo Library/Photo Researchers; D56 (b) Robert Williams and the Hubble Deep Field Team (STScI) and NASA; D58 Dr. Robert Mallozzi of Universtiy of Alabama/Huntsville & NASA; D58-D59 Chris Cheadle/Stone; D59 Tony Freeman/PhotoEdit; D60 Courtesy of Julio Navarro/University of Victoria; D63 (l) Lynette Cook/Science Photo Library/Photo Researchers; D64 (t) Andre Jenny/Unicorn Stock Photos; D64 (b) Dennis Johnson/Folio;

Unit E

Unit E Opener (fg) Alvis Upitis/The Image Bank; (bg) Tim Crosby/Liaison International; E2 Jim Steinberg/Photo Researchers; E2-E3 Charles Krebs/The Stock Market; E3 H. Armstrong Roberts; E7 (b) NASA; E10 (bg) Ron Chapple/FPG International; E10 (bi) Dr. E. R. Degginger/Color-Pic; E12 Charles D. Winters/Photo Researchers; E14 Spencer Swanger/Tom Stack & Associates; E15 (c) Phil Degginger/Color-Pic; E16 Dr. E. R. Degginger/Color-Pic; E16-E17 Tom Pantages; E17 Tom Pantages; E18 Yoav Levy/Phototake; E19 Yoav Levy/Phototake; E20 NASA; E23 (t) Tom Pantages; E23 (c) Yoav Levy/Phototake; E23 (b) Tom Pantages; E24 Horst Desterwinter/International Stock Photography; E25 (t) Dr. E.R. Degginger/Color-Pic; E25 (i) Norman O. Tomalin/Bruce Coleman, Inc.; E28 Joe Sohm/Photo Researchers; E29 (t) Doug Martin/Photo Researchers; E29 (b) Gary A. Conner/PhotoEdit; E30 (i) Glenn Photography; E30 Geoff Tompkinson/Science Photo Library/Photo Researchers; E34 Jan Taylor/Bruce Coleman, Inc.; E34-E35 Pete Saloutos/Stone; E35 Dr. E.R. Degginger/Color-Pic; E36 Superstock; E38 Lee Snider; E40 (t) J & L Weber/Peter Arnold, Inc.; E40 (b) Dr. E.R. Degginger/Color-Pic; E41 (Top to bottom) Joe Towers/The Stock Market; E41 (photo 2) Christopher S. Johnson/Stock, Boston; E41 (photo 4) Telegraph Colour Library/FPG International; E41 (photo 6) George Haling/Photo Researchers; E42 (li) Richard Laird/FPG International; E42 (b) Wesley Hitt/Stone; E44 Yoav Levy/Phototake; E48 Michael Monello/Julie A. Smith Photography; E50 (t) © PhotoDisc; E50 (bl) Mel Fisher Maritime Heritage Society, Inc.; E50-E51 (bg) Michigan Molecular Institute; E51 Michigan Molecular Institute; E52 (i) UPI/Corbis; E52 Mitch Kezar/Phototake; E56 (t) Sal Dimarco/Black Star/Harcourt; E56 (b) Courtesy of Jefferson Lab;

Unit F

Unit F Opener (fg) David Zaitz/Photonica; (bg) Stone; F2-F3 NASA/Photo Researchers; F3 (t) NASA/ Science Photo Library/Photo Researchers; F3 (b) Jean-Loup Charmet/Science Photo Library/Photo Researchers; F6 (l) Tony Duffy/Allsport Photography; F6 (c) Pascal Rondeau/Allsport Photography; F6 (r) Allsport Photography; F7 (tr) Spencer Grant/PhotoEdit; F7 (cr) Spencer Grant/PhotoEdit; F10 (b) David Young-Wolff/PhotoEdit; F12 (l) Myrleen Ferguson/PhotoEdit; F12 (r) Mark E. Gibson; F18 Superstock; F19 David Young-Wolff/PhotoEdit; F20 (b) Stephen Frisch/Stock, Boston; F21 (t) Novastock/PhotoEdit; F21 (ct) Tony Freeman/PhotoEdit; F21 (b) Tony Freeman/PhotoEdit; F24 NASA; F25 NASA; F26 (i) Dr. Ephraim Fischbach; F26 NASA; F30-F31 Chris Butler/Science Photo Library/Photo Researchers; F31 (t) Stephen Dalton/Photo Researchers; F31 (b) Mike Cooper/Allsport Photography; F32 (bl) E & P Bauer/Bruce Coleman, Inc.; F35 David Madison/Bruce Coleman, Inc.; F36 (i) Mark E. Gibson; F36-F37 Lee Foster/Bruce Coleman, Inc.; F38 (bl) Michael Newman/PhotoEdit; F40 A. C. Cooper LTD/Harcourt; F40-F41 Ed Degginger/Bruce Coleman, Inc.; F41 NASA; F42 Tony Freeman/PhotoEdit; F43 Mike Yamashita/The Stock Shop; F44 CP Picture Archive (Chuck Stoody); F46 Tom McHugh/Photo Researchers; F49 Erich Lessing/Art Resource, NY; F51 Scala/Art Resource, NY; F52-F53 Lawrence Livermore National Laboratory; F53 (t) Lawrence Livermore National Laboratory; F53 (b) Michael Rosenfeld/Stone; F54 NASA; F58-F59 Scott Warren; F59 (b) M. Zhilin/M. Newman/Photo Researchers; F60 Jan Butchofsky-Houser/Dave G. Houser; F62 (l) Duomo Photography; F62 (c) William R. Sallaz/Duomo Photography; F62 (r) Steven E. Sutton/Duomo Photography; F63 (t) Gary Bigham/International Stock Photography; F63 (ti) Ken Gallard Photographics; F63 (bl) Stevn E. Sutton/Duomo Photography; F63 (br) Duomo Photography; F64 Greg L. Ryan & Sally Beyer/AllStock/PNI; F66 Peter Menzel; F68-F69 Phil Degginger/Bruce Coleman, Inc.; F69 (tr) Ontario Science Centre; F69 (br) Phil Degginger/Bruce Coleman, Inc.; F72 (tr) Michael J. Schimpf; F74 (bl) Stone; F76 (l) E.R. Degginger/Bruce Coleman, Inc.; F76 (c) E.R. Degginger/Bruce Coleman, Inc.; F76 (r) Tony Freeman/PhotoEdit; F78 (tl) Tim Beddow/Stone; F79 (tr) Danila G. Donadoni/Bruce Coleman, Inc.; F80 Norbert Wu/Stone; F82 Chuck O'Rear/H. Armstrong Roberts, Inc.; F86-F87 Peter Cade/Stone; F88 (t) Michael Keller/The Stock Market; F88 (bl) The Granger Collection; F88 (bc) Kevin Collins/Visuals Unlimited; F88 (br) American Stock Photography; F89 (tl) Corbis-Bettmann; F89 (bl) Michael Nelson/FPG International; F89 (r) Lester Lefkowitz/The Stock Market; F90 (i) Dr. Jean M. Bennett; F90 Diane Schiumo/Fundamental Photographs; F94-F95 Jeff Hunter/ The Image Bank; F95 (t) Science Photo Library/Photo Researchers; F95 (bl) James King-Holmes/ Science Photo Library/Photo Researchers; F95 (br) Ron Chapple/FPG International; F96 Cary Wolinsky/Stock, Boston/PNI; F98 Billy E. Barnes/PhotoEdit; F99 (tl) Gary Conner/PhotoEdit; F99 (tr) Bill Aron/PhotoEdit; F99 (br) Myrleen Ferguson/PhotoEdit; F100 (tl) Tony Freeman/PhotoEdit/PNI; F100 (br) David Young-Wolfe/PhotoEdit; F102 Jim McCrary/Stone; F104 (b) Wendell Metzen/Bruce Coleman, Inc.; F104 (i) Mark E. Gibson; F105 (tl) Keith Gunnar/Bruce Coleman, Inc.; F105 (tr) Mark Newman/Bruce Coleman, Inc.; F105 (c) Tony Freeman/PhotoEdit; F106 (c) Claus Militz/Okapia/Photo Researchers; F108 (bl) Myrleen Ferguson/PhotoEdit; F110 (t) Alan L. Detrick/Photo Researchers; F110 (b) Cameramann International; F111 (t) Nicholas de Vore III/Bruce Coleman, Inc.; F111 (c) Andrew Rakoczy/Bruce Coleman, Inc.; F111 (b) Glen Allison/Stone; F112 (tr) Lockheed Space and Missile Co., Inc.; F114 (t) © Corel; F114-F115 Mark E. Gibson; F115 (t) M.E. Rzucidlo/H. Armstrong Roberts; F115 (b) Andy Sacks/Stone; F116 (l) Drew Donovan Photography; F116 (r) Stan Ries/International Stock Photography; F120 (t) Courtesy of the National Science Center's Fort Discovery; F120 (b) Courtesy Associated Electric Cooperative, Inc.;

Health Handbook

R16 (c) Tony Freeman/PhotoEdit; R16 (br) David Young-Wolff/PhotoEdit; R17 (t) Myrleen Ferguson Cate/PhotoEdit; R17 (b) David Young-Wolff/PhotoEdit; R19 Tony Freeman/PhotoEdit; R45 (br) © PhotoDisc; R45 (bl) PhotoDisc;

All other photos by Harcourt photographer listed below, © Harcourt: Weronica Ankarorn, Victoria Bowen, Eric Camden, Digital Imaging Gorup, Charles Hodges, Ken Kinzie, Ed McDonald, Sheri O'Neal, Terry Sinclair & Quebecor Digital Imaging.

Illustration credits - Tim Alt B14-15, E15, E16-17, E39, E40, E41, F84; Scott Angle R44, R45; Art Staff C66; Paul Breeden A94; Lewis Calver A8, A9, A10, A11, A12, F78-79; Mike Dammer A57, A117, B85, C29, C57, C89, C125, D31, E53, F55, F117; John Dawson B38, B78-79; Eldon Doty A31, A57, A117, B57, C29, C125, D31, E53, F55, F117; Pat Foss A85, A117, B21, B57, B85, B117, E31, F27, F91; George Fryer C44, C46; Patrick Gnan F22, F65, F77, F78; Dale Gustafson B7, F64, F70-71, F72, F106; Nick Hall C102, C106; Tim Hayward A40; Jackie Heda A16, A17, A18, A19, A20, A25, A26; Inklink F20-21; Roger Kent A95, A100, A101, B44; Mike Lamble C16, C17, D6-7, D8, D9, D33, D55, F34-35, F48-49, F50; Ruth Lindsay B8-9, B92-93, B106-107; Lee MacLeod A27; Alan Male A79, A80, B43; MapQuest C75, C96; Janos Marffy C22, D15; Colin Newman B76-77, C110-111; Sebastian Quigley C64-65, C67, C72, C73, C75, C76, D14, D16-17, D38-39, D40-41, D46, D47, D48-49, F7; Rosie Sanders A102, A103; Mike Saunders A50, A51, C9, C10, C14-15, C18-19, C24 ,C31, C50-51, C98-99, C105, C118-119, F8; Andrew Shiff A31, B21, B117, C87, D61, E31, F27, F91; Steve Westin C42-43, C45; Beth Willert A24.